W9-ARB-765

EARLY CHILDHOOD EDUCATION SERIES

Leslie R. Williams, Editor   **Millie Almy, Senior Advisor**

Outdoor Play: Teaching Strategies with Young Children
JANE PERRY

Embracing Identities in Early Childhood Education: Diversity and Possibilities
SUSAN GRIESHABER & GAILE S. CANNELLA, Eds.

Bambini: The Italian Approach to Infant/Toddler Care
LELLA GANDINI & CAROLYN POPE EDWARDS, Eds.

Educating and Caring for Very Young Children: The Infant/Toddler Curriculum
DORIS BERGEN, REBECCA REID, and LOUIS TORELLI

Young Investigators: The Project Approach in the Early Years
JUDY HARRIS HELM and LILIAN G. KATZ

Serious Players in the Primary Classroom: Empowering Children Through Active Learning Experiences, 2nd Edition
SELMA WASSERMANN

Telling a Different Story: Teaching and Literacy in an Urban Preschool
CATHERINE WILSON

Young Children Reinvent Arithmetic: Implications of Piaget's Theory, 2nd Edition
CONSTANCE KAMII

Supervision in Early Childhood Education: A Developmental Perspective, 2nd Edition
JOSEPH J. CARUSO & M. TEMPLE FAWCETT

The Early Childhood Curriculum: A Review of Current Research, 3rd Edition
CAROL SEEFELDT, Ed.

Leadership in Early Childhood: The Pathway to Professionalism, 2nd Edition
JILLIAN RODD

Inside a Head Start Center: Developing Policies from Practice
DEBORAH CEGLOWSKI

Uncommon Caring: Learning from Men Who Teach Young Children
JAMES R. KING

Teaching and Learning in a Diverse World: Multicultural Education for Young Children, 2nd Edition
PATRICIA G. RAMSEY

Windows on Learning: Documenting Young Children's Work
JUDY HARRIS HELM, SALLEE BENEKE, & KATHY STEINHEIMER

Bringing Reggio Emilia Home: An Innovative Approach to Early Childhood Education
LOUISE BOYD CADWELL

Major Trends and Issues in Early Childhood Education: Challenges, Controversies, and Insights
JOAN P. ISENBERG & MARY RENCK JALONGO, Eds.

Master Players: Learning from Children at Play
GRETCHEN REYNOLDS & ELIZABETH JONES

Understanding Young Children's Behavior: A Guide for Early Childhood Professionals
JILLIAN RODD

Understanding Quantitative and Qualitative Research in Early Childhood Education
WILLIAM L. GOODWIN & LAURA D. GOODWIN

Diversity in the Classroom: New Approaches to the Education of Young Children, 2nd Edition
FRANCES E. KENDALL

Developmentally Appropriate Practice in "Real Life"
CAROL ANNE WIEN

Quality in Family Child Care and Relative Care
SUSAN KONTOS, CAROLLEE HOWES, MARYBETH SHINN, & ELLEN GALINSKY

Using the Supportive Play Model: Individualized Intervention in Early Childhood Practice
MARGARET K. SHERIDAN, GILBERT M. FOLEY, & SARA H. RADLINSKI

The Full-Day Kindergarten: A Dynamic Themes Curriculum, 2nd Edition
DORIS PRONIN FROMBERG

Assessment Methods for Infants and Toddlers: Transdisciplinary Team Approaches
DORIS BERGEN

(Continued)

Early Childhood Education Series (title nonnm...

The Emotional Development of Young Children:
Building an Emotion-Centered Curriculum
MARION C. HYSON

Moral Classrooms, Moral Children: Creating a
Constructivist Atmosphere in Early Education
RHETA DeVRIES & BETTY ZAN

Diversity and Developmentally Appropriate
Practices
BRUCE L. MALLORY & REBECCA S. NEW, Eds.

Understanding Assessment and Evaluation in
Early Childhood Education
DOMINIC F. GULLO

Changing Teaching, Changing Schools:
Bringing Early Childhood Practice into Public
Education—Case Studies from the Kindergarten
FRANCES O'CONNELL RUST

Physical Knowledge in Preschool Education:
Implications of Piaget's Theory
CONSTANCE KAMII & RHETA DeVRIES

Caring for Other People's Children:
A Complete Guide to Family Day Care
FRANCES KEMPER ALSTON

Family Day Care: Current Research for
Informed Public Policy
DONALD L. PETERS & ALAN R. PENCE, Eds.

Reconceptualizing the Early Childhood
Curriculum: Beginning the Dialogue
SHIRLEY A. KESSLER & BETH BLUE SWADENER, Eds.

Ways of Assessing Children and Curriculum:
Stories of Early Childhood Practice
CELIA GENISHI, Ed.

The Play's the Thing: Teachers' Roles in
Children's Play
ELIZABETH JONES & GRETCHEN REYNOLDS

Scenes from Day Care
ELIZABETH BALLIETT PLATT

Raised in East Urban
CAROLINE ZINSSER

Play and the Social Context of Development in
Early Care and Education
BARBARA SCALES, MILLIE ALMY,
AGELIKI NICOLOPOULOU, &
SUSAN ERVIN-TRIPP, Eds.

The Whole Language Kindergarten
SHIRLEY RAINES & ROBERT CANADY

Children's Play and Learning
EDGAR KLUGMAN & SARA SMILANSKY

Experimenting with the World: John Dewey and
the Early Childhood Classroom
HARRIET K. CUFFARO

New Perspectives in Early Childhood Teacher
Education: Bringing Practitioners into the Debate
STACIE G. GOFFIN & DAVID E. DAY, Eds.

Young Children Continue to Reinvent
Arithmetic—2nd Grade
CONSTANCE KAMII

The Good Preschool Teacher
WILLIAM AYERS

A Child's Play Life: An Ethnographic Study
DIANA KELLY-BYRNE

The War Play Dilemma
NANCY CARLSSON-PAIGE & DIANE E. LEVIN

The Piaget Handbook for Teachers and Parents
ROSEMARY PETERSON & VICTORIA FELTON-
COLLINS

Promoting Social and Moral Development in
Young Children
CAROLYN POPE EDWARDS

Today's Kindergarten
BERNARD SPODEK, Ed.

Visions of Childhood
JOHN CLEVERLEY & D. C. PHILLIPS

Starting School
NANCY BALABAN

Ideas Influencing Early Childhood Education
EVELYN WEBER

The Joy of Movement in Early Childhood
SANDRA R. CURTIS

OUTDOOR PLAY

teaching strategies with young children

JANE P. PERRY

Foreword by Doris Pronin Fromberg

Teachers College, Columbia University
New York and London

Published by Teachers College Press, 1234 Amsterdam Avenue, New York, NY 10027

Library of Congress Cataloging-in-Publication Data

Perry, Jane, 1955–
    Outdoor play : teaching strategies with young children / Jane P. Perry ; foreword by Doris Pronin Fromberg.
       p. cm. — (Early childhood education series)
    Includes bibliographical references and index.
    ISBN 0-8077-4118-3 (cloth : alk. paper)—ISBN 0-8077-4117-5 (pbk. : alk. paper)
      1. Play—California—Berkeley—Case studies. 2. Outdoor recreation for children—California—Berkeley—Case studies. 3. Education, Preschool—Activity programs—California—Berkeley—Case studies.
    4. Social interaction in children—California—Berkeley—Case studies.
    I. Title. II. Early childhood education series (Teachers College Press)
  LB1140.35.P55 P47 2001
    372.13—dc21   2001027495

ISBN 0-8077-4117-5 (paper)
ISBN 0-8077-4118-3 (cloth)

Printed on acid-free paper
Manufactured in the United States of America

08 07 06 05 04 03 02 01   8 7 6 5 4 3 2 1

Contents

Foreword *by Doris Pronin Fromberg*   vii

Preface   ix

Acknowledgments   xv

1. OUTDOOR PLAY   **1**

A Play Area as an Ecology   3

The Play Yard as a Complex Learning Environment   5

Pretend Play with Peers   8

The Roles of the Teacher   16

Teacher Profiles   19

The Classroom Teaching Culture   24

2. NEEDLES   **26**

Initiation and Negotiation Phases of the Episode   27

Enactment Phase of the Episode   31

Review of the Episode   38

3. MAKING A NEW ROAD   **42**

Initiation and Negotiation Phases of the Episode   43

Enactment Phase of the Episode   45

Review of the Episode   52

4. "THE DAM IS BREAKING"   **54**

Initiation Phase of the Episode   55

Negotiation Phase of the Episode   56

Enactment Phase of the Episode   56
Review of the Episode   65

5. TWO GUYS   **68**

Initiation and Negotiation Phases of the Episode   69
Enactment Phase of the Episode   72
Review of the Episode   79
The Primacy of the Play Episode   82

6. TEACHER STRATEGIES IN THE PLAY YARD   **83**

Indirect Coordination of the Ecology   84
Direct Intervention in the Play Episode   92

7. THE SOCIAL AND CULTURAL ORGANIZATION
   OF THE PLAY YARD   **104**

Play Routines Serving the Peer Culture   105
The Teacher Culture and Expectations for Valued Behavior   114
Conclusion   117

References   **119**

Index   **123**

About the Author   **128**

Foreword

This book is born into an era of fundamentalist political forces that advocate for an academic-transmission curriculum, a narrow conception of teacher-proof curricular scripts and linear paper- and electronic-workbook materials, high-stakes standardized testing of isolated skills, and a limited image of education as based in an indoor classroom. In sharp contrast to the present political climate, Jane Perry studies the outdoor play of young children and the role of professional early childhood teachers.

Jane Perry uses case material and vivid images that are drawn from a clearly guided conceptual framework advocating quite a different worldview. The genetic roots of this book lie in the progressive, holistic, child-centered view of the significance of play not just in the classroom but beyond—in the outdoors. Outdoor play becomes an antidote to linear education. It is also a location in which to observe the power of play and to assess the professional judgments of early childhood teachers. This book reminds the adult reader about the reasons for children to play.

It is a book that celebrates the power of a professional teacher to form professional judgments and interact respectfully with children. It is a book that brings to life the dynamic processes involved in socio-dramatic play, that helps the reader appreciate the three-dimensionality represented by the two-dimensional page. It is a celebration of the birth and rebirth of the child's play themes as eloquent representations of socio-cultural and personal-cultural experiences.

In another dimension, the ethnographic gestation that helped this book to coalesce reflected a collaborative effort between the author-ethnographer and the other teachers. By sharing specific data and collaboratively interpreting events, the teachers, and the author as teacher-researcher, came to crystallize their understanding of the role of the outdoor physical and social environments in children's development. An understanding of the dynamics of learning outdoors is also relevant to indoor learning; indeed in less hospitable climates the indoor environment may be the only available place for children to engage in socio-dramatic play.

The author provides enough detail to reveal both the complexity and accessibility of ideas that make it possible to transform professional perspectives into professional judgments. For example, the author models specific questioning strategies and presents alternative ways in which a teacher might intervene during specific phases of play. The details create a degree of suspense usually found in novels: I came to care about Lawrence, for example, and wanted to find out what happened to him.

There is a great deal to learn about early learning and professional education in the space between the context of the book and the context of current policies. The space in which to learn is filled with the empowerment of children as creative players and teachers as collaborative builders.

Doris Pronin Fromberg
Hofstra University
January 2001

Preface

I have chosen to study teaching strategies from the perspectives of both the teachers and children at the Harold E. Jones Child Study Center, of the Institute of Human Development, University of California, Berkeley. As the research for this book progressed, the teaching staff helped me to create a language that I use both in understanding outdoor teaching styles and in advocating the importance of the play yard in any early childhood classroom.

When I initiated this study, I was not yet a teacher at the school. I approached the head teacher with my interest in developing a framework for teachers to consciously understand how to support self-directed play in the play yard. She expressed interest in the idea. Her classroom had been using the findings of Scales (1987) to support the children's developing interactive competence. The teachers were eager to clarify their intuitive framework. I was offered a work-study teaching position in the classroom. As it turned out, I never left. I continue to teach in this classroom, refining my skills and thoughts every day as the children, deeply embedded in the culture of their peer play world, unpredictably challenge the satisfaction of my findings. In a very important sense, this book represents a work in process, as I am buoyed by the unpredictable freshness of children vividly at play.

THE CLASSROOM

At the time of my study, the classroom included, as it does now, 24 children and between four and five teachers at any one time. Then a half-day afternoon nursery school program, the classroom now functions as a full-time child care facility for 3 and 4 year olds. The program has retained its focus on the physical and social features of the classroom environment and how those environmental features support the development of the whole child. In addition to the ecological elements of the classroom, we also offer a rich array of teacher-guided activities. We base teacher-guided activities on three major themes. First, the children's transition to school from home and prior care experiences; second, the children's awareness of themselves physically and as a member of both a family and a peer group; and third, the children's participation in a wider appreciation of the worlds of ancestry and cultures.

The children in this book are predominantly from middle- and upper-class families. The classroom is ethnically mixed. The names used in this study are not the children's real names. For the specific group of children enrolled during the spring of this study's videotaping, many children were approaching the age of 5 and often played in same-sex groups; therefore, selection of episodes of play was gender-specific. Gender specificity also related to the teacher. The episodes of pretend play with teacher support recorded for the male teacher most always involved the play of boys. In addition, both of the teachers' support of play involving girls most often involved content relating to turn-taking, friendships, and the like. In these cases, the play themes were associative in nature, rather than sociodramatic, more often than not. Since I was interested in pretend peer play, associative play was not included in my analysis.

While this study does not include gender differences in its analysis, it appeared from the videotape record that girls tended to play without appeal or need of teacher support when involved in pretend peer play. In other words, pretend peer play by the girls was integrative, progressive, and of long duration independent of teacher involvement exclusive of setup. This book is therefore more about teachers supporting boys playing together.

The children in this book include Lawrence, pervasively curious about the games of others; Raymond and Matthew, tentative players practicing at being "naughty"; Danny, Seth, and Chris, experienced master players willing to share their expertise through observation; Warren and Carl, adept rough-and-tumble players; and Dora and Marta, who get embroiled in what it means to be a girl or a boy and how girls and boys act with one another. This book features two teachers as well: Karen and Ken.

OBSERVATIONS OF TEACHERS SUPPORTING PRETEND PLAY WITH PEERS

I collected observations in three ways: videotapes of activities in the play yard, audiotapes of reviews of the videotaped material by the teachers, and my own field notes. I used videotape data to document what two trained teachers, Karen and Ken, did and said during children's outdoor pretend play with peers. The videotape equipment was set up on the perimeter of the yard. Two unidirectional microphones hung, one over a sand play area and one over a climbing structure area, each from a guide wire. In addition to the hanging microphones, the teacher also wore a clip-on remote microphone. Videotaping was from a fixed angle and a fixed focal length. All audiovisual equipment was in full view of the children, teachers, and parents.

Videotaping occurred in the spring. I chose to film on consecutive days to capture the progression of children's peer play themes across many days. Videotape recording began one half hour before opening to capture teacher setup activities and ran until an end-of-the-day inside time. Total recording time for each day was 2¾ hours. Each teacher was filmed for a total of 4 days, with Karen and Ken teaching on alternate days.

Each teacher participated in individual interviews as they viewed selections from the videotaped record. I based selections of activity for screening on (1) identified group pretend play episodes involving teacher facilitation and (2) other interactive activity between the children and/or the teacher that appeared to stand out as important, puzzling, or difficult to grasp (Johannessen, 1987). Setup activities in the play yard for that day were always included in the viewing selections. Following Erickson (1986), I encouraged the teacher to stop the videotape and/or comment on any action recorded. Each teacher was asked the reasons for the particular setup of the area and intentions in acting in the ways recorded on the tape. In a final viewing organized at the request of both Karen and Ken, the two teachers were able to observe and comment on each other. This occasion proved to be a rich source for analysis. Coming as it did at the end of the individual viewings, both teachers were well equipped to comment on their differing styles, and the consequences such style differences appeared to have on the children's kind of play as seen on the film. The teachers clearly gained facility both in understanding their teaching style and in being able to describe their style after having viewed the videotapes.

Following the teacher screening of the videotape records, I made a final selection for microanalysis of the longest episodes of pretend play where either the teacher verbally intervened at least once or was invited to participate by at least one of the children involved in play. I did not include episodes of long duration when a teacher was not involved or was involved solely in conversation or nonverbal interaction not related to the pretend play. For a detailed discussion of videotape coding, refer to Perry (1989).

My aim in the microanalysis was to document, first, the complexity of interactions so noted in the literature on pretend play with others, and second, how the teacher maintained the duration of pretend play. This microanalysis included the audiotapes from the teacher screenings as well as my own field notes.

Field note information included four sources. I recorded an account of all *unusual events* occurring during the taping schedule, including classroom circumstances, technical aspects of the taping procedure, and weather. I documented *staff conversations* during formal meeting times as well as informal gatherings. I made *methodological notes* regarding my reflections on the procedures of the research. And finally, I recorded *theoretical notes* regarding thoughts on the meaning of teacher and child interactions in the yard. As noted by Corsaro (1985), the chief advantage to this recording convention is that it allows the researcher to separate out different types of information in the data while insuring that the data are tied to the specific interactive contexts in which they occurred.

THE ORGANIZATION OF THE BOOK

Chapter 1 introduces the play yard as a set of discrete expectations and cues for learning within which children grapple with complex social and communicative demands. I organize children's self-directed ritualized play in a sequential framework of initial *initiation* of play with another, *negotiation* of roles and themes, and *enactment* of the theme as it develops and perhaps transforms. I introduce the two experienced teachers, Karen and Ken, as they talk about organizing, observing, and promoting outdoor pretend play. I also introduce the classroom teaching culture as a negotiating chip in the life of the play yard. Chapters 2 through 5 provide anecdotal evidence of children who are working hard to establish friendships and feel in control of their own thoughts and actions. I use the framework of initiation, negotiation, and enactment to analyze how the teacher supports self-directed pretend play with others. The anecdotal chapters exemplify how two teachers with the same philosophical orientation differ in their goal of maintaining the duration of an episode of play. Chapter 6 outlines teacher decisions and strategies used to create, preserve, and protect outdoor areas for play, as well as to sustain interactions while honoring the children's self-direction. I maintain that by intervening from inside the thematic context of the children's play, teachers cultivate the children's own learning perspective. In conclusion, in Chapter 7, I use the anecdotal evidence to illuminate both the children's and the teacher's expectations for interacting in the yard. I describe the peer play routine as a distinctive ritual children use to seek out affiliative reassurance. I describe the teaching culture of my classroom and the value Karen and Ken placed on children interacting together. I emphasize the importance of points of rupture in peer play episodes as opportunities to confer acknowledgment, and negotiate meanings between the peer and teaching cultures.

With the information presented in this book, teachers will have the concepts and terms to use in explaining the strengths of outdoor play to themselves, to fellow teachers, and to administrators, parents, and the public. As such, this book is an explicit effort to advocate for children by providing language to identify the sequence of a play episode, the intentions of playmates when involved in play, and the strategies teachers use to support children's learning experiences during outdoor play.

Acknowledgments

I am indebted to Barbara Scales, who taught me, first, how to notice and follow children's perspectives as they play, and second, how to help others honor the intention behind the act. I am forever touched by her mentorship and the dignity she instills in the classroom. The willingness of the two teachers, Karen and Ken, to join me in minute analysis of word and gesture was generous in time and spirit, and I am grateful for their collaboration. I also thank the children, families, teachers, and staff of the Harold E. Jones Child Study Center, whose participation, reflections, and support are a foundation for this book.

At Teachers College Press, Susan Liddicoat provided invaluable support by combining astute and clear editorial comments with next-step suggestions that reinvigorated my initiative. I am grateful to the anonymous reviewers whose response and suggestions improved this book immeasurably, and to Leslie Williams for her enthusiasm for my work.

My deep appreciation goes to Anne Perry, Doug Reisner, Mary Hutchison, Michelle Sherry, and Rebecca Tracy for wading through early drafts and providing down-to-earth reactions and suggestions, to Robin Peters-Petrulewicz and Carol Higgins for invaluable technical assistance, and to photographers Lynn Bradley and Bob Devaney for capturing life outdoors.

And to my husband, Bob Devaney, for his music, quick humor, and impeccable storytelling throughout the course of this project.

1   *Outdoor Play*

Credit: Bob Devaney

I am quietly moving amongst different play groups in the yard, informing the children that it is time for snack. As children and teachers both return from washing their hands, I hear a group of boys already gathered at an outside snack table: "It's teacher time! It's teacher time! Teacher time!" they call out, laughing at their joke.

WHAT IS "TEACHER" in the play yard when children's play is so absorbingly self-directed? Imaginative play with friends includes running from danger and collecting dirt, water, and carefully plucked leaf ingredients for complex baking recipes. Vivid negotiations over turf occur during ball and vehicle play. Shrill oscillating-toned cries signal entrance to the yard and availability for play. Feigned swoons leave children motionless amidst the fast-moving agenda. Some watch the play of others, sometimes from the height of a climbing structure, while others plunge deeply into the fray of frenzied fantasy. Some taunt relent-lessly. Some are often taunted when they inadvertently challenge the peer protocol of the yard.

This book is about how a teacher supports children in self-directed outdoor fantasy play with peers. National accreditation resources (see, for example, Bredekamp & Copple, 1997; Bronson, 1995; Dodge & Colker, 1992) are clear that developmentally appropriate practice involves the teacher's use of play as the medium through which the young child learns best. This book shows what it looks like for a teacher to support learning through outdoor play.

I focus on children interacting with each other. While individual children emerge in the book as interesting characters, I look at the progress of children-in-interaction. I expect that preschool children will be able to initiate an interaction with another child independent of the teacher. I expect that the children will be able to negotiate not only a theme to the interaction, but related roles once the theme is established. I also expect that the children will elaborate on the theme as the interaction is enacted in play. I use the experiences and reflections of two teachers, Karen and Ken, to exemplify how a teacher can consciously prepare, encourage, and coordinate children's outdoor pretend play with each other. I believe that self-directed fantasy play in the yard is an essential feature in the social and emotional development of young children. I use the perspective of children and teachers in one classroom to tell stories about life in the play yard. The children can tell their stories of outdoor play by themselves. This first chapter can be read either prior to the storied Chapters 2 through 5, or after, as a way to highlight the rich complexity of play in the yard.

What *are* children intending when they play so vigorously outside? Clearly children are doing more than exhausting energy. They have focused attention to very specific and usually recurring actions and themes. Their play themes are generally self-generated, since the yard has less thematic suggestions than, for example, the inside playhouse. Children seek out the yard to create fantasies amongst themselves. As Diane Levin (1998) astutely notices, children may even be directed out of doors by us teachers who see their behavior as being an "outside game" (p. 353). The flexibility of play cues allows for a distinct expression and manifestation of the world of young children from their own cultural play perspective. As any teacher in a play yard will attest, it is outside that the most vivid cultural manifes-tations of the peer group can appear: in hierarchical rankings of members, in possession of stationary and non–stationary objects, and in the claim-ing and relinquishing of friendships, to name a few. The play yard is a learning environment where teaching strategies occur alongside the spontaneous strategies of the peer culture.

The educator Barbara Scales (1984) describes how teachers guide children in a play-based program:

> Features [of the setting] are designed to interest, stimulate and challenge the children's spontaneous play, exploration and discovery. A consequence of this emphasis is that ecological variables are stressed. In this way, peer play can be maintained indirectly, thereby preserving the child's autonomous choice of pace and mode of involvement with peers, adults, or activities and materials of the program. (p. 43)

The boys' joke in calling snack time "teacher time" is evidence that they, too, are aware of when they experience autonomy in the classroom and when they do not. "Teacher time" demonstrates a playful sense of creativity and rebellion in renaming, while also establishing "teacher" as an authority figure. Scales offers a clue to understanding what the term *teacher* means. She looks at the teacher as one in a cluster of features in the classroom environment that guide children's autonomous activities. Scales highlights the interaction that children have with their classroom environment, which in the play yard includes interaction with climbing apparatus, a sand area, space for fast-paced movement, as well as other children and at least one adult. It is children-in-interaction that is observed. Doris Fromberg (1999), after reviewing current research on play, concurs. According to Fromberg, looking at children's play involves studying "a relational phenomena" where what is observed is dynamic, nonlinear, and episodic. Sounds like an accurate description of the play yard in action! Teacher supervision of outdoor play means looking at the interaction between children and the features of their play setting.

A PLAY AREA AS AN ECOLOGY

Scales (1987) has another clue for understanding supervision in the play yard. She defines the environment of the classroom as a series of ecologies. An ecology is an area that suggests certain kinds of activities. In the early childhood classroom, an ecology is an activity area. Preschool and early elementary education programs have traditionally used defined areas to support children's active, independent involvement with learning materials: the block corner, the playhouse, writing tables, the reading corner, the large climber, the sand area, the swings, and manipulative areas. Areas are set up to communicate expected behavior clearly. Materials are easily accessible. The materials have a defined use. Each area is protected or delineated in some fashion to focus and protect the activity. Usually each area has a name, making reference to and negotiations about the area possible. In addition to materials, an ecology also includes the children and teachers and how they use the play area. The teacher coaches beginning players in the appropriate use of materials or apparatus, often modeling behavior and language that can be successfully used in times of negotiation and turn-taking. The children interpret ecological cues, oftentimes in innovative ways. Such interpretive innovation gives an ecology its dynamic quality.

A play ecology presents teacher goals by communicating expectations about intended behavior. Researchers in a variety of early childhood classrooms have described how ecologies support children's active involvement (see, for instance, Cazden, 1983; Cook-Gumperz & Corsaro, 1977; DeVries, Haney, & Zan, 1991; King, 1992; Paley, 1992; Pellegrini, Huberty, & Jones, 1995; Scales, 1987; Trawick-Smith, 1994). As Scales aptly identifies, expectations for learning are communicated in ecologies through three types of cues:

1. The suggestive features of the objects, materials, and available areas
2. What children naturally enjoy doing with certain materials in certain areas
3. The shared history of play by children in an area

All three cues communicate a message to children regarding what is intended or expected in a particular area as they coordinate their different perspectives. Some areas have quite explicit cues. The suggestive features leave little to negotiate, and children are familiar with the themes and what roles accompany those themes. The inside playhouse, for example, in a very explicit manner, cues for cooking activity with its small dishes, cups, pots, pans, stove, tables, and chairs. The explicitness of the cues also signals kitchen roles and themes. Most children, in other words, are familiar with what people do in a kitchen, especially if there are props like plates, a few pots, and stirring spoons. These highly familiar objects easily cue for standard familial repertoires of cooking, eating, and feeding without much need for explanation. A child can move quickly into such a play area and begin stirring from a pot. Another child can sit at the table and be served. Further, the child stirring the pot will probably assume a caretaker role. The context of these two children's play has been established from the explicit cues of the ecology without any spoken words. Their play interaction also becomes a vivid piece of information to be recalled when they are next in the playhouse.

The familiarity of the ecology as a play setting appears to facilitate more creative and competent play (Aureli & Coecchia, 1996; Ramsey & Lasquade, 1996). The ecology, by providing suggestive features of daily life, capitalizing on the routine of what children enjoy doing with materials, and defining a structured area where children have a shared history, creates a "script" that helps organize children's knowledge (see, for instance, Fein & Wiltz, 1998).

Various play areas in the preschool make differing demands on the child's communication and socialization skills based on the degree of explicitness of the play area cues. The explicit cues of the playhouse present less of a demand on children to communicate and negotiate play roles and themes. The playhouse can therefore be an opportunity to promote play in children with less communicative and socialization skills, because they can rely on the conventional nature of such cues. However, argues Trawick-Smith (1998), when props are too realistic, the realism tends to limit interpersonal interaction:

> The uses of realistic props do not require as much explanation or justification, do not demand the same level of agreement among players. The forms and functions of a shopping list or a grocery cart are obvious; no ongoing negotiations are needed about what these represent. In contrast, transforming a wooded rod into a fire hose requires some debate, since so many alternative symbolizations can be imagined. (p. 245)

When cues are open-ended and children are involved in negotiating idiosyncratic personal symbols, interactions by necessity become more complex.

THE PLAY YARD AS A COMPLEX LEARNING ENVIRONMENT

With less explicit cues than those inside the classroom, outdoor play challenges children's abilities to interpret (Scales, 1987). The suggestive features of the objects and materials are flexible and can be adopted for a number of roles in a number of themes. With less explicit ecological areas, the shared history of play in the area is a prominent cue. In my classroom, I have certainly observed that what was played yesterday in the sand area is on children's minds when next they enter the area. When children move outside to the sandbox or the climbing apparatus where behaviors like digging or climbing are apparent but the themes and roles are not as explicit, the challenge to communicative abilities increases. Without explicit thematic structure, the play yard is ripe for imaginative interpretation. Making a new road in the sand area one day can trigger repeat play amongst playmates on successive days. According to Scales, when children playing together are given the opportunity to autonomously make sense of the environment, play interactions are more cohesive.

Teachers in my classroom would concur with Fromberg (1999), who finds that when children play with low-specificity toys, their play is more interactive, includes more mutually shared play themes, and includes less interruption than when children play with high-specificity props. Hartup, French, Laursen, Johnston, and Ogawa (1993) observe that in "open-field" play contexts, characterized by open-ended free choice play outside of the classroom, children seek to "manage their conflicts in ways that minimize risk to their interactions" (p. 446). Children are motivated to play for longer duration. Trawick-Smith (1998) suggests that in open-field ecologies, children are "more likely to be persuasive rather than demanding, to compromise, and to resolve disputes without aggression" (p. 242). The flexibility of ecological cues allows preschool children to interpret. In making sense of their play area during pretend play, children's interactions are more cohesive.

Outdoor play by its very nature involves children making complex distinctions between pretend and real as group running, chasing, fleeing, and wrestling erupt in both playful fun and primitive expressions of emotion. Teachers in the play yard will be regularly helping children to encode and decode the social signals that distinguish rough-and-tumble play and aggression (Pelligrini & Smith, 1998). Teachers support children's social competence in the play yard by focusing on how children are using and interpreting play ecologies. Two ecologies from my own classroom play yard are a sand pit and a climbing structure, both of which are under one teacher's supervision.

The sand pit is located in the middle of the yard and marked by a cement lip around its outer rim (see Figure 1.1). Attached to the far end of the sand pit is a small deck structure, in the center of which is a large oak tree. Adjacent to one side of the sand pit is the major entrance and exit corridor for the yard from the inside classroom. The children in the sand pit play with various props such as toy cars and trucks, rakes, buckets, and shovels, and also use water available from a spigot. The children develop hand-eye coordination while manipulating and organizing props, sand, and water. They engage in pretend play based on themes suggested by the objects in the sand area. As they invent and develop games, they interact with playmates to arrive at consensual rules about how the game is to be played.

The climbing structure, pictured in the opening of this chapter, is located along the back periphery of the yard. It is marked by a ground covering of tan bark, which separates it from a cement portion of the yard.

FIGURE 1.1: The Sand Pit Ecology: An Area That Suggests Certain Kinds of Activities.

Credit: Lynn Bradley

The climbing structure includes a 7-foot high, two-tiered deck supported by brightly painted poles from which attach a number of slides, chutes, sliding poles, and ladders. There is a fair amount of traffic flow past this area. Activity centers around large muscle movement, usually in the context of pretend play with others. Due to its height, the deck provides a degree of privacy, which allows a variety of familial/house themes to develop. Other role play themes include superhero and animal play. This area can comfortably accommodate four to eight children. This was a very active and generally noisy area. By observing children in self-directed play in ecologies such as the sand pit or large climber, teachers can assess whether area cues are presenting learning goals for the classroom in complement with the abilities and interests of the children.

Implicit in the discussion of the play yard ecologies is the notion that the indoor classroom and the play yard present a continuum between the more quiet, focused activities of the inside and the more noisy and self-defined features of the play yard. Table 1.1 contrasts the play yard with the inside classroom, in a rudimentary way. While vigorous noisy play will certainly erupt inside, and focused, task-oriented play will occur outdoors

TABLE 1.1: Contrast Between the Inside Classroom and the Play Yard

CATEGORY	INSIDE CLASSROOM	PLAY YARD
Suggestive features of the ecology	Explicit cues	Flexible cues
Physical space in ecologies	Confined	Spacious
Quality of play	Quieter, task-oriented, teacher-generated as well as self-directed	Noisier, physically vigorous, self-generated
Children's ability to interpret	Children rely on explicit cues to guide themes and roles	Children invent themes and roles in open-ended, flexible ecologies
Demand on communication and socialization skills	Less demand	More demand

as well as indoors, conceptually the inside classroom and the yard create a continuum that offers children available options for their self-generated play.

PRETEND PLAY WITH PEERS

Between the ages of 3 and 5 years old, children engage in more pretend play with each other than in any other form of play (Rubin, Fein, & Vandenburg, 1983). One way teachers support learning and development is through encouraging such group fantasy play. Pretend play with peers provides the opportunity for complex cognitive and social development.

The researcher and teacher trainer Sara Smilansky (1968) studied group fantasy play in the classroom. She finds that competence in pretend play with others is linked to children's language skills; their skills in thinking comparatively about people, objects, and information about their world; and skills in problem solving. Smilansky (1968) defines six features of pretend play with peers that mark its sophistication:

1. Children match play behavior with adopted pretend role.
2. Children use make-believe objects to substitute for real objects and use verbal utterances to represent action.
3. Children describe make-believe action in the course of coordinating their game.
4. Children persist in a play episode for at least 10 minutes.
5. The play involves at least two children engaged in pretending.
6. Children verbally interact in the course of the play, usually to clarify or to negotiate.

Smilansky's work demonstrates that the structure of pretend play with peers can become increasingly complex during the preschool years when children take on fantasy roles that coordinate their actions with others. Children shift between reality and fantasy. They need language skills to communicate and negotiate theme development, roles, materials, play partners, and play space. The ability to take turns in pretend play is a landmark feature in children's developmental progression. Whereas in toddler play, turn taking tends to be the simple repetitive duplication of ideas and actions of the other player, in the preschool years turn taking allows children to elaborate on play themes and practice taking the perspectives of others.

Language skills clearly play an increasingly important role in play when children are attempting to negotiate different perspectives. Children's awareness and use of specific language is a prerequisite for decision making and negotiations involved in group problem solving. "But *I* want to be the squirrel," protests one child after roles have already been picked. "Well, there can be two," offers the first squirrel. "O.K.!" Psycholinguist Susan Ervin-Tripp (1983) points out the importance of language learning in peer interactions:

> These activities not only make possible the child's display of language knowledge, but create some conditions for the child to learn to understand new words and new constructions, to imitate, to recall, and to extend what is known. Learning derives not just from speaking but from hearing language used in a context where the meaning is obvious and where the learner is interested enough in what is going on to pay close attention. That is why play contexts are so much more efficient than traditional classrooms. (p. 12)

Pretend play with peers not only reflects the child's current level of functioning, but also can frame continued development through consolidation and practice of newly emerging skills. Particularly in the play yard, where ecologies are more flexible to innovative thematic interpretation, pretend play with peers offers significant linguistic and cognitive challenges.

Pretend play with peers requires sophisticated social skills. Children juggle playmates, toys, and space. Children are challenged to communicate the progress of the play theme as it transforms from reality to fantasy. Children hold notions of fantasy and reality in mind at the same time. Children in group-fantasy play must make mutual agreements about what to pretend to be, what to pretend to do, where to pretend to be, what to pretend that various objects are, as well as manage the various disagreements along the way. The Soviet psychologist Lev Vygotsky (1967) argued that it was just such social challenges, prompted by the children's desire to maintain peer interaction, that stretched cognitive functioning beyond usual levels. In fact, according to Vygotsky (1978), it is at this social level where development first appears, manifesting itself individually in the child following the social gain.

Pretend play with peers in the yard is important because it allows for complex learning involving language skills, perspective taking (understanding another's point of view), representational thinking, problem solving, turn taking, and the ability to interpret environmental cues, while at the same time retaining an autonomous, child-directed focus. Especially in light of the entry into the culture of elementary school, exhaustive opportunities for pretend play with peers during the preschool years is preparative. Pretend play with peers provides children with experience in directing their own learning, gives children the background needed to know what it means to be a friend, and provides them with repeated experience in how to read ecological cues. The best way for teachers to create a supportive environment that encourages the complexity of learning inherent in outdoor play with peers is to notice how children independently organize socially and then to complement children's natural capacity to establish social relations.

Children's Play as Peer Culture

Children acquire skills and knowledge from the world they share with their peers and with adults. Upon examining play in the yard, it is clear that acquisition of skills and knowledge occurs when children actively participate in exploring, constructing, and thereby making sense of their world. Children organize and interpret information from their world as they play, often in each other's company. Children's intellectual understanding progresses through stages of ability. While adults can guide, nurture, protect, and challenge children in their developmental progress, children will perceive and organize their world in ways that are qualitatively different from adults.

The sociologist William Corsaro (1985, 1997) sheds light on the idiosyncratic way that children relate to each other as they learn, especially in the play yard. According to Corsaro, children's social development cannot be explained merely as internalizing adult skills and knowledge. As children construct meaning from their everyday lives, they actively create a series of unique peer cultures that address their concerns. Corsaro believes that social development in young children is a process of both interpreting the adult world and producing a peer culture uniquely suited to the world of play with each other. The peer culture of young children includes common activities, rules, rituals, and themes based on their sense of their everyday lives as well as incorporating their representation of the adult world as they understand it. Outdoor play provides ample evidence of children's early peer culture. Inclusion in play is often based on imagined roles: "You have to be a dinosaur to be in this hole." Adult authority is challenged: "It's nap time! Let's hide!" Past episodes of play together figure prominently in negotiations: "Hey guys! I got it! Let's play horsies. 'Member that time we did that?" Territory is righteously claimed: "You can't come up here!" Games of flee and chase frequently erupt, and rough-and-tumble wrestling, cuffing, and feigned fear are like waves wafting over the yard.

Based on his own work and the work of others, Corsaro finds two consistent themes in the initial peer cultures of young children. The first he calls *communal sharing* or *social participation*, which is the strong desire to be affiliated with other playmates. The second theme he calls *control*, which is the persistent attempt by children to challenge and gain control over their lives. Corsaro (1985) sees the peer culture as a "joint or communal attempt by the children to acquire control over their lives through the establishment of a collective identity" (p. 75). Together, these two themes of the peer culture offer children social allegiance in the context of living in the powerful world of adult authority.

Peer-Culture Rituals and Routines

Peer-culture rituals and routines are easy to notice. Corsaro (1979) found that interactions are regulated by appeals to friendship. Play interactions often begin by a request to acknowledge affiliation: "We're friends, right?" Asking for an acknowledgment of friendship also occurred when children wanted access into an ongoing game: "Let's say we're twins,

O.K.?" Corsaro (1985) found, however, that 75% of such appeals were met by resistance: "No, I don't need a twin!" This resistance establishes a precedent for vigilance if play with others is desired. Termination of a play episode can occur without warning or recognition, leaving a playmate unpredictably without a partner. Such vigilance and unpredictability together create a quality of fragility to peer interactions.

Children respond to the feeling of fragility with play routines intended to assure participation and some measure of control. Friendship is the integrative glue that helps to preserve the play interaction. Appeals to friendship are a device both to gain access to and protect peer play (see Figure 1.2). Children's peer play routines, such as the various forms of flee and chase so common in the play yard, provide an integrative function by coalescing the peer group. Allegiance and a desire for affiliation is revealed as children make their often primitive attempts at negotiating as independent players. Wild running games are the children's way of feeling connected.

FIGURE 1.2: The Desire to Be Affiliated Is One of Two Themes of the Preschool Peer Group.

Credit: Bob Devaney

Games that create alliance can also have an exclusionary function in children not yet ready to imagine a theme beyond being chased by an unwitting "bad guy" (see, for example, Paley, 1992; Trawick-Smith, 1988, 1992, 1994; Van Hoorn et al., 1999). The teacher Karen Gallas (1998) reflects on the vividness of the children's social agenda in her own classroom, noting that their struggles to make sense of control and power dominate:

> As the years progressed, my concept of "teaching well" altered and good teaching became more than believing that I was covering important curricula and that children were mastering subject matter. The social and political began to loom large as driving concerns. Children's desires for affiliation, their need to play and create new worlds, pressed in. Issues of power and entitlement, of alienation and failure, of silent or silenced complicated the process. (p. 2)

So strong are children's efforts to make sense of the issues of power and control that their themes create a pervasive "subtext" in her classroom.

Gregory Bateson (1976), looking at the play of both animals and humans, sheds light on how players communicate the message or signal for "this is play." An exaggerated stance or pose, a play voice, a change in voice tone, or a verbal request are some of the ways children signal their intention to play. The vocal quality to play yard games is therefore due in part to children cueing each other that "this is play." The way in which playmates understand and respond to such "this is play" overtures can be an area of negotiation during peer play. Teachers in the yard will often find themselves clarifying children's intentions. "I think Mark wants to play with you. He keeps running after you."

Observing nursery school play, Jenny Cook-Gumperz (1978) has found that once involved in a play interaction, affiliation continues to be a powerful chip in the peer culture. Introducing a new play idea into an ongoing event, for example, requires children to secure a "warrant" or agreement from companions. "Pretend this is my road, O.K.? O.K.?" "O.K." Children use a change of voice tone to signal or mark a shift in theme (see Cook-Gumperz, 1981), and they use register differences during pretend play to indicate different roles (see, for example, Anderson, 1977). Teachers in the play yard will notice highly ritualized and repetitive behavior like screaming, accompanied by running and feigned aggression and fear emerging when language skills are not accessible or available, under new circumstances, or when a playmate is shy or feeling threatened by a challenge like the entrance of another playmate.

Scales (1987) has found that self-directed play with others not only supports the development of social competence, but that there is a correlation between the duration of self-directed play interactions and the children's own independent negotiating skills. Scales's work confirms what I had found in other resources: pretend play with others is an important component of children's social and emotional development. However, Scales is adding a new piece to the picture. She finds that the longer the game, the more children show evidence of negotiating skills. This makes sense. Children have a strong desire to be affiliated, and will work hard to keep the game going. When children are involved in making sense of play-area cues, their social skills are more integrated. Self-directed play offers an integrative glue precisely because children are actively interpreting rules and expectations for each other. Here the primacy of the peer culture is revealed. When children are encouraged to autonomously make sense of their world, as they do when they play with each other using rituals and routines established as a cultural group, their social skills are more cohesive.

Autonomous play occurs more readily in outdoor ecologies in part because play yard ecologies are more flexible to innovative interpretation. Children work hard in the play yard because they are motivated to be affiliated. Issues of power, control, and access emerge as children make sense of flexible ecological cues. Children use a variety of rituals and routines to integrate their games. Vigorous play emerges in the play yard where children are distinctively social even as they negotiate the play of chasing, fleeing, and wrestling. When children playing together are given the opportunity to make sense of the environment autonomously, play interactions are decidedly more cohesive. And children more than likely will be engaged in pretend play with each other. Teachers support children's social competence by focusing on how children are using and interpreting play ecologies. The teacher in the play yard determines whether learning-area cues are clear and make sense for the children as they play. What do teachers look for as children independently organize themselves in the play yard?

Sequence of Pretend Play with Peers

Scales has identified three phases in the sequence of an episode of play with peers. *Initiation* involves some proposal by a child accompanied by an acknowledgment from another child. This condition of initiation or proposal of some mode of activity is very familiar to any preschool teacher in the play yard. "Let's play dinosaurs, O.K.?" "We're twins, right?" "I'm the father and you're the baby." "You wanna play sharks?" In fact, initiation is so standard in peer play that it makes identification of the beginning of a game quite obvious. A familiar form of initiation of an episode of play begins with the use of a question such as: "We're friends, right?" followed by an acknowledging "Right!" If players have a history of shared play together, such acknowledgment can be quite subtle, such as a simple exchange of smiles or an idiosyncratic yell or screech. At this point children are deciding whom to play with.

Once players are identified, the episode proceeds to a *negotiation* phase when children decide what they are playing. Again, a question is often a familiar device to prompt such negotiation, and teachers observing peer play will often hear such dialogue: "We're making cakes, right?" "Yeah, and this is our house, but we don't have a Mommy." "Pretend we're hiding from the bad guys, and these are our bullets, O.K.?" "Up there is where we sleep, right?" While such explicit negotiating is often heard, it is not necessary if the theme is obvious, as it might be with players who have a long history of shared play together. Here the influence of the teacher begins to emerge. The ecology in which the play occurs includes cues, which help to establish the theme more clearly. The teacher's creation of an ecology for play, be it trucks and shovels in the sand area, or a cluster of milk crates suggesting some kind of enclosure, can expedite peer play when the teacher is aware of the suggestive features of objects and materials, what children naturally enjoy doing with materials, and the shared history of past themes amongst playmates. The ecologies serve a teaching function by complementing the themes of affiliation and control so prevalent in preschool peer play.

Once playmates have negotiated a theme to their game, the play episode proceeds to the *enactment* phase, where the play theme is expanded, developed, and/or transformed as the game progresses. Players may change ecologies, expand or lose playmates, or remain quite settled for a long duration. Players can be independent in their negotiation during this phase or they may need help from the teacher when the play interaction breaks down.

Teachers can use their understanding of the sequence of play yard games to promote the duration of children's play interactions. In this way, teachers support complex, independent interactions. Teachers set up and maintain learning areas, noticing how their setup represents cues for thematic play. When breakdowns occur in children's games, teachers help them to clarify their play intentions and choices. Teachers mediate disputes by offering words to use. Sometimes teachers also play in the ecologies and, by example, offer themes and roles. Sometimes children respond to area cues clearly and as teachers expect. Sometimes teachers find themselves reacting to unanticipated behavior, struggling to promote focus when enthusiasm seems out of control. They confer with each other, trying to make sense of the children's world in the yard and their roles in supporting the children's learning and development.

THE ROLES OF THE TEACHER

Two girls are crouching low. One exclaims in a hushed whisper as she wipes the sand flat: "It's buried now!" The other adds more sand. "That's good." A third playmate arrives, questioning the proceedings. She is rebuffed with annoyance: "A *grave*! We're making a *grave*!" A fourth child crawls from an adjacent spot in the sand, driving his truck into the foot of one of the grave diggers. The teacher moves close to the truck driver, informing him gently: "Don't drive your truck into them, please."

Children in the play yard are making sense of themselves in social groups: recreating experiences from their family lives, from the life of the classroom, and from information received from text and media. They play vigorously, exploring physical and interpersonal space in often fast-paced, highly vocal, tactile games. Looking at the literature, I find that educators and researchers vary in their recommendations for how, when, and even if, to support children during self-directed peer play.

Van Hoorn and her colleagues (1999) promote play as the centerpiece of developmental learning in the classroom. Teachers are guided in their facilitation of children's play and learning by four principle strategies:

1. Appreciating the child's view of experience and materials
2. Functioning as a keen observer
3. Preparing the physical environment and daily schedule for play
4. Recognizing the variety of learning contexts in which children construct meaning and gain knowledge.

Jones and Reynolds (1992) and Reynolds and Jones (1997) believe children learn by constructing their own knowledge through play. The more competently children play, the more clearly they will understand their world. Teachers provide the opportunity for children to play and to develop through play. Teachers organize the environment, mediate disputes during points of conflict, and with beginning players, assume the role of teacher as player. As children master independent play, the teacher supports constructive learning as a play watcher who observes, reflects, builds hypotheses, and plans.

Smilansky (1968, 1990) defines teaching strategies as playing with children. Following her work is Trawick-Smith (1994). Both scholars advocate playing with children as one means of facilitating learning. Smilansky has developed teacher facilitation techniques during pretend play with peers to specifically support children who are lacking in play experience. Facilitation techniques include suggesting a theme, offering language, extending play ideas, modeling play behavior using objects and assumed roles, and changing the physical environment. Trawick-Smith argues that despite evidence like Smilansky's on the benefits of playing with children, teachers do not spend enough time in direct play interaction with children. He encourages being an unobtrusive player, offering comments and suggestive elaborations while refraining from becoming a leader of the action. In unobtrusive play, the teacher enriches children's play, promotes social competency, and enlightens herself or himself to the lives of her or his students.

Drawing on my own research and that described above, as well as my teaching experience, I have developed the following framework for characterizing the roles of teachers in supporting children in self-directed play in the play yard:

1. *The teacher as organizer.* Teachers organize ecologies in the play yard to create challenges and activities for the children. We emphasize the clarity of ecological cues to promote specific developmental goals. The play yard is designed and set up to replicate traditional indoor activities so that intellectual, social, and affective development can be integrated with the children's outdoor needs and interests. Teachers offer an array of outdoor activities, including domestic and social role play, constructive play, tactile and sensory experiences, fine and gross motor activities, and play in art, science, math, and language arts (see Figure 1.3). A designated area features teacher-guided projects. The play yard offers room for children to watch each other play. Arrangements in area ecologies are predictable and familiar and capitalize on the children's interests. The setup of a play ecology accommodates a range of skills and abilities, so that when children accomplish a level of play, they can return with newly developed expertise to master more complex tasks. Teachers introduce new materials and play opportunities following the children's autonomously directed progress. Play opportunities and materials are based on the background, interests, and readiness for new accomplishments.

2. *The teacher as observer.* Teachers position themselves in adjacent supervision areas of the inside classroom and play yard so that the children can freely move among inside and outside areas at their own inclination. Having organized play ecologies with some idea of how children use materials, teachers now observe how children interpret play area cues. What do the children find enjoyable about the availability and organization of materials in specific areas? What themes emerge that the children will recall as a shared history when next in the area? Is there anything about the area that confuses the progression of peer play?

FIGURE 1.3: Teachers Offer a Variety of Outdoor Activities, Including Language Arts.

Credit: Lynn Bradley

Teachers in my classroom collect "slices of life" observational narratives on each child during floor time. These teacher observations are reviewed in staff meetings to discover how the child is interpreting cues for learning in inside and outside areas.

3. *The teacher as promoter.* Learning areas, when organized and maintained, do much of the teachers' work as promoters of self-directed play in the yard. Teachers promote interactions in small groups by encouraging face-to-face play: a small manipulative table with two play spots facing each other, an extra-wide slide or gym mat that allows for full-body embracing, a tire swing negotiated by the children that facilitates role identification ("I'll be the pusher!"), as well as the vividness of eye contact. Teachers are alert to a balance in the number of children across the areas of supervision. Teachers protect interactive play by avoiding overcrowding so that the children's burgeoning social and linguistic competence is not overtaxed. Teachers keep an eye out for those children who naturally initiate interactions, those who are currently learning by watching, and those who would benefit from side-by-side play. Teachers notice children who are disengaged and uninvolved with either materials or playmates, and invite playmate interaction: "Raymond, come and see what Marta is doing with the blocks." Teachers make explicit their expectation that all children need experience in peer play: "It's time to find someone to play with. Let's see what's cooking in the sand kitchen." Teachers offer play language, voice, and actions to model behavior for novices.

These three roles are a way to look at how teachers support children's outdoor pretend peer play by encouraging autonomous exploration, experimentation, and learning in small groups. To get a vivid look at teachers in action in the play yard, I introduce two teachers.

TEACHER PROFILES

Karen and Ken are two experienced teachers in my study. Though different in style, they both support self-directed peer play in the yard.

Karen

Karen's interaction into an ongoing play activity occurs most often by using a verbal reference to some detail of the children's thematic activity. I call this kind of strategy interacting *within the play theme*. If the teacher observes what children are playing, or knows that the stack of milk crates is actually their "refrigerator," the teacher can refer to such fantasy material when directly speaking to children. By referring to the children's fantasy play structures, locations, or adopted roles, the teacher figuratively "moves into" the play theme for a moment and accepts it as the current reality. The effect on children's play, and often on their willingness to comply with requests, is discussed in Chapter 6. Karen frequently refers to the play theme when interacting with children (e.g., "that's their jail"). On some occasions, such thematic references are for the benefit of a child on the sidelines.

Karen does not directly intervene as a player in any of her interactions. I therefore differentiate Karen's style from Smilansky's (1968) play intervention technique, which Smilansky denotes as being within the play interaction. Karen's style functions to acknowledge the play theme while remaining a commentator rather than a player.

Karen's observational stance provides her with rich information about who is playing with whom, who wants to play with whom, which play themes are currently being adopted, and which materials and areas of the yard are being used to act out such themes. As Karen observes, she is continually framing her observations vis-à-vis a developmental perspective. In one particular conversation early in the research, Karen explained that she felt her developmental perspective had come more from her master's credential program than from accumulated experience as a teacher at the center. She finds that this developmental perspective helps her make sense of occurrences during teaching. She told me, "Children will work on intonation, for example, and you can tell from their odd phrasings what they are working on." Her developmental framework appears as an overlay to the immediacy of the moment-to-moment interactions she observes in the yard. Karen's style is so observational, in fact, that it was not until she and I viewed the videotapes of her teaching that I was able to account for Karen's perspective during interactive teaching-learning events. During these screening sessions, Karen was quite talkative in regard to her thoughts during the actual taping. She was able to provide ample evidence for the fact that an observational stance can function to developmentally frame and assess the progress of interactions as they occur.

Karen's style is marked by a nondirective, observational stance, which provides her with rich information regarding the context of events in the yard. From such a stance, she clearly projects the impression of acknowledging and respecting the interests and perspectives of the children not only by allowing interactive activity generally independent of any direction from her, but also by being keenly aware of and acknowledging the children's play themes.

During a screening interview, Karen describes her interactive style as "coming and going":

That whole thing, coming and going, coming in close and stopping and going back out, and checking. And when I come in and when I don't come in. To *me*, *that's* what I'm really doing when I'm out there . . . I'm always debating, am I going to say something, how am I gonna say it? I can be sweeping away, sweeping away and never look up, but there will be a sound and something that will trigger me to look up and know something is going on. And then, I'll check it out for a minute, and I'll either come in closer or maybe just watch it from where I am. All that hinges on what's happening at the moment. Is somebody getting hurt, is somebody gonna fall in the near future so I should be over there right now, or is this something that while I'm going over there maybe they'll work it out as I'm on my way over, which sometimes happens. I'll get halfway there, and it's all worked out, and I just won't bother. I try and help them do it themselves and keep trying to get out of it as quickly as I can, so that they can take it over. But yet if they're not going to take it over, I'll stay there and help until I feel it's worked out.

Fromberg (1999) describes pretend play with peers in a similar fashion: "The negotiations of social play in particular appear to involve an oscillating process between what you expect in somebody else's behavior and what you find" (p. 33). Karen is well aware that children operate in a dynamic, nonlinear context during play and she attempts to match their context with her style. It is impossible to know for sure whether Karen is accurate in her determinations of context. However, the fact that she is rarely, if ever, corrected by the children when she refers to their play activities lends credibility to her understandings.

Karen facilitates small group play by preparing the ecologies in her area. She arranges physical space in defined ways so that play spots are marked. She capitalizes on the suggested features of materials. In this way Karen maintains an indirect role in supporting pretend play. She steps back to follow the play action as it evolves from the children's own pace and mode of activity.

Ken

One of the most distinguishing features of Ken's style in the yard is the frequency with which he explicitly tends to promote small group pretend play opportunities either by suggestion of a play theme or by direct involvement as a player in the interactive play. Ken usually suggests quite specific imagery: "You might want to use this pole as an escape route from enemies."

Ken's setup arrangements are especially suggestive. Ken organizes ecologies to create "a place where things can happen." In an early screening interview, Ken characterized his creation of "place" in terms of both visual and geographic cues. These cues define actual physical, spatial boundaries in the sand and suggest an area "where you can do things," as, for example, by raising or lowering heights in the sand pit by digging out trenches, tunnels, and hills. For Ken, depending on the quality of such setup arrangements, his created "places" can suggest the allusion to specific themes: "safe/unsafe, civilized/uncivilized. My kind of set-up will pull for a place where you can do things. It's just a theme, and it's just mine. But they make it on their own level, like space play. Space is so flexible and of a different world." Ken's suggestive arrangements allow flexibility for interpretation. Outer space play is flexible because it can include all sorts of invented space tools, props, and eventual landing sites. It is not as tied to specific cues as is the inside playhouse, for example, and can therefore launch into any number of uncharted fantasies.

Ken is quite conscientious in terms of preparing the yard for thematic play before the children arrive. As a teacher he is hesitant, however, to admit that he is adopting a specific and conscious strategy in this regard: "Oh, if you are talking about timing, and setting up the yard, and thinking about that, I do a lot of that. When I am home, I will make drawings. You can always come up with rationalizations, but it's usually not so conscious, just visual play." Ken was hesitant in our discussions about his style because of his reluctance in seeing himself as a teacher with specifically defined teaching goals. During preliminary negotiations with Ken to secure his informed consent to participate in my research, Ken first voiced reservations. I had asked him what he thought being a teacher meant. For Ken, being a teacher means "someone who takes grades, rates performance, presents formal curriculum." In the play-based world of the play yard, Ken's conceptualization of himself as a teacher is incongruous to him. I explained that one of the important goals of this program is the preservation of play. When I stressed that the head teacher had chosen both him and Karen for their expertise in supporting self-directed learning, Ken appeared visibly relieved. He immediately related some "especially fun" times when he had been able to set up pretend play events with the children.

Throughout this study, Ken persisted in resisting the notion that what he is doing is actual teaching. During a screening interview of the videotapes of his teaching, Ken again stressed that he felt he was not teaching anything specific, but rather he was "like a big kid, who could help the other kids do things." For Ken, the teacher role is reserved for nonplay circumstances: "And when someone got hurt, for example, I would move into the teacher role and bandage them up." Being a promoter and supporter of play activities, therefore, is not included in Ken's definition of teacher.

Ken nonetheless acknowledged his success in supporting fantasy play, attributing his success in part to the program's acceptance of teacher time spent in observing, and identifying the children's perspective or agenda:

> I don't feel I have an agenda of my own, but I look at the children's agenda. I don't have to sit down and teach them numbers and concepts. This is why I want to be here. I get a lot of pleasure in talking to kids about what they are doing. I don't have to worry about what I am teaching. There are never any expectations on me as a teacher in regards to 'teaching' them, so I can be myself. And I just happen to enjoy watching their fantasy play. To the extent that I can facilitate that, and help them do it on their own in whatever way I do, the better I feel about what I'm doing.

In addition to suggesting possible thematic play options, Ken also participates directly in ongoing play interactions with children. This is the specific activity he is referring to when he describes himself as a "big kid." Prompted by a question from Karen, who was interested in how Ken both initiated and stepped out of interactive activity with the children, Ken described his participation this way:

> I start with lots of direction. And I have to watch to see how they are holding it on their own. I only step out when I see they are carrying it on their own. And then I step back in quickly when I see they need help, when I see it's breaking down.

One specific consequence of Ken's involvement as a play partner in the children's play is his regular verbal and nonverbal participation in the immediate action of the evolving interaction. Ken will often provide commentary on his actions. Compared to Karen, whose teaching intentions became apparent only when she spoke about her thoughts during video screenings, Ken's strategies appear in-the-moment, spontaneously, as both he and the children work together within the play event.

These two teachers exhibit definite differences in how they guide children's outdoor play. Karen is the *teacher as observer*. Her style results in less direct interaction with the children than Ken's more active interventions as the *teacher as organizer and promoter*. Karen facilitates children's peer play based on their own devices for initiation. Ken acts as a model for interactive play, initiating actively with the children. Karen's observational stance provides her with a rich appreciation of each child's level of development in play with peers. Ken's interactive stance results in his role as a player. Ken's information derives from an in-the-moment experience of being part of the spontaneous development of a play sequence, though he readily admits to elaborate preparations of the play ecology. The childrens' play may have a spontaneous script, but the area has been thematically structured prior to initiation.

THE CLASSROOM TEACHING CULTURE

Teachers in my classroom use group meeting times to sing, act out dictated stories, read from topical books, and review school news, but also to surface peer group themes as they arise. For example, how do we keep each other safe at school? What is a friend? Is it O.K. for your friend to play with someone else? What does it mean to be a good guy? What is a bad guy? What do you think bad guys really want? These topics are ongoing discussions, usually being left in-process to be picked up later as all of us make sense together in the classroom. At these times of discussion, I am most aware that even as I facilitate the children's pretend play together, I nonetheless come from my own cultural perspective as a teacher.

The profiles of both Karen and Ken suggest that there are some overriding beliefs that both teachers, while different in style, nonetheless share. Like children, who have developed their own set of practices that make up the peer culture, teachers also have their own perspective, called the classroom teaching culture (see, for example, Erickson, 1986; Erickson & Mohatt, 1982; Florio & Walsh, 1980; Philips, 1982; Schultz, Florio, & Erickson, 1982). The classroom teaching culture, like any other cultural organization, they argue, includes rules of etiquette that define what is appropriate and inappropriate under certain circumstances. Susan Philips (1982) has defined the social organization of the classroom teaching culture: events such as circle time, cleanup time, reading, and so forth, where each event "time" has particular and definable ways of interacting. As any teacher knows, the label of reading "time," juice "time," or group "time" is a signal to children for a particular set of expectations for behaving and interacting. Heath (1983) confirms that the school environment communicates messages for expected behavior, and also that the children themselves help to shape those cues. Gallas (1998) notes the clash of culture evident in her classroom:

> Observations that describe points of rupture in the life of the classroom, points of confusion, missteps, and even chaos give us access to the points

when teacher intention as it is embodied in a method encounters the prosaic world of children and daily life. (p. 17)

The classroom teaching culture is clearly evident in traditional, teacher-directed classrooms. My analysis of teacher's and children's interactions in the yard suggests that the inside classroom teaching culture can be expanded to include interactions outdoors as well. I look at the initiation of an occurrence of pretend peer play as my starting point, noticing points of rupture, confusion, and missteps, and activity appearing to stand out as important, puzzling, or difficult to grasp. It is in these moments of mutual negotiation between children and teachers in the yard where the two cultures can best be seen. The four anecdotal play episode chapters that follow are examples of the interaction between the peer culture and the classroom teaching culture. Together, the chapters are a glimpse into the world created by the children and their teachers as they navigate their way in the play yard.

2   *Needles*

Credit: Bob Devaney

MATTHEW AND RAYMOND have been playing on the slide in a game the teachers refer to as "being naughty." This play activity is seen frequently with children in later preschool years and involves doing naughty or "bad" things that are against the rules of the school. This game is familiar to teachers in my classroom, who understand it as something maturing preschoolers do to clearly identify a sense of themselves as separate from those around them. Teachers refer to this type of activity as "testing."

Just 15 minutes prior to the initiation of this episode, Raymond had been teased and chased by another group. While Raymond said he did not like what they were doing, and even threatened to tell the teacher, the group continued without concern, even challenging Raymond by saying, "Go ahead, tell the teacher!" Raymond, for whatever reasons, did not tell Ken.

This episode is typical for teachers supervising outdoor play. It involves repetitive chasing between two play groups, each with its own grievances about the other. While both groups use their complaints as fuel for continued chasing, neither party seems at all interested in either ceasing or leaving the action. In fact, while the teacher is very often called upon to settle such disputes, the same activity will continue after teacher intervention. Due to the persistent nature of this activity, teachers in my classroom had begun to wonder if they were themselves being drawn into the game by the children in order to play some role. They noticed that while their attention to the manifest grievances identified by the children seemed to answer some need of the players, the game nonetheless continued. In the following episode, Ken attempts to clarify play intentions for those involved. In a review of the episode at the end of this chapter, I will further elaborate on Ken's strategies as well as discuss the children's use of rejection of another as a primitive initiation into pretend play.

Players in this episode include Raymond, age 4 years, 4 months; Matthew, age 5 years, 7 months; and Lawrence, age 4 years, 6 months. The episode lasted for 18 minutes and occurred on the large climber. The large climber includes a wide exit and entry slide, adjacent to which is a ladder, usually for entry. Under the slide is another ladder, used almost exclusively for climbing up to the platform from which the slide descends. There are bars for hanging, adjacent to the slide, as well.

INITIATION AND NEGOTIATON PHASES OF THE EPISODE

Raymond and Matthew have just come from having juice. Raymond walks over to the hanging bars, in front of the climber. He says something to Matthew, who is still eating. Matthew listens to Raymond, then climbs up the slide. Raymond is flipping his leg over one of the hanging bars in front of the slide area.

Raymond finally calls: "Matthew!"

Matthew responds without looking as he walks up the slide. "What?"

Raymond repeats his stunt. "Lookit!"

Slipping, Matthew misses Raymond's stunt. "What?"

Raymond again struggles awkwardly to lift his leg in order to touch the top of the hanging bar. ". . . Look at this."

Matthew nods in approval from the top of the slide. "Mmm!" With Matthew's nod and verbal marking of approval, the episode is formally initiated. Raymond has initiated a "look at me" game. Matthew, while polite, is noncommittal. Raymond's good friend, Lawrence, now enters. Raymond and Lawrence often play together during after-school hours. Their families share a similar cultural background, though Lawrence, unlike Raymond, is learning English as a second language.

Lawrence faces Raymond and smiles. Raymond swings his arms at Lawrence and Lawrence moves back. Lawrence moves around to one side of Raymond and Raymond approaches Lawrence and pushes him away forcefully. Lawrence backs off but faces Raymond. Neither boy shows any visible emotion. Lawrence now voices his concern. "Don't. Don't push—!"

At the same time, Raymond begins to speak over Lawrence's remarks. He continues emphatically after Lawrence is finished. "No! Go away!" Raymond appears ready to play with one partner but finds the addition of a second partner threatening, especially when the second playmate is a good friend.

Pretend play with peers is a function of children's keen desire to make sense of their world in independent play together. In an early childhood classroom, children make sense of classroom learning cues in the company of others. The psychologist George Herbert Mead (1934) has written that it is through playing together that the development of self occurs. Raymond is learning to differentiate between the "I" or the spontaneous self in action and the "me" or social self in relation to others. In time, with the cognitive gains made in repeated opportunities to play with others, he will learn to coordinate multiple perspectives simultaneously. But for now, Lawrence's arrival as a second partner in the social equation challenges Raymond's social and language skills. Because his level of social development makes it difficult to create a group that includes both Matthew and Lawrence, he acts aggressively toward the newcomer. This challenge of allegiances in interactions is a regular feature of young children's play and will be seen in the following episodes as well. Children desire social participation. They try to gain access to interactions when uninvolved. However, when involved, children are aware of the fragility of their interactions with others, and are equally concerned with protecting their play from the interests of others (Corsaro, 1985, 1997).

Raymond continues demonstrative physical and verbal gestures to refuse Lawrence's overture to play. Lawrence is persistent, following Raymond up the slide. Raymond turns to face Lawrence and kicks in his direction. Lawrence gets off the slide and walks in the direction of Ken, who has been observing another area of the yard.

Matthew has been standing on top of the slide, munching on his snack and watching periodically. Seeing Lawrence talking to Ken, Raymond calls out to Matthew: "Let's hide. Let's hide. Let's hide under the slide." Lawrence's appeal to Ken has prompted Raymond to suggest a "hide from

the teacher" theme. Matthew and Raymond run under the slide and up
the ladder to the slide platform, cementing Raymond's suggestion in mutual
acknowledgment.

Functioning as a short-handed cue, "let's hide" is a signal that identifies a familiar play theme in the peer culture—namely, a shared threat. This
game works only when playmates run from something. Corsaro (1985)
discusses running with "feigned fear" as a persistent theme in young children. So familiar in the peer culture of young children, the theme is evoked
nearly "spontaneously," according to Corsaro:

> There is *no direct negotiation* about when to begin the routine, what each
> child is supposed to do, or when the routine is to end. The mere pres-
> ence of a possible threatening agent . . . is transformed into an approach-
> avoidance routine. (p. 223, emphasis in original)

Lawrence has sought out Ken for help in his dispute with Raymond.
"Teacher. Raymond's *kicking*."

Ken interrupts Lawrence in order to suggest that Lawrence negotiate
his own dispute. "You know, then I would tell him that," instructs Ken. "If
he is doing something you don't like, then I'd use words." Lawrence is
actually requesting help at initiating play with Raymond, though his complaint is about aggression. Lawrence has been attracted to an established play
group that he would like to join, in the company of Ken. Lawrence adopts
an elegant entry technique for initiation here. He "tells on" Raymond, his
desired playmate. Lawrence wants Ken to initiate contact with Matthew and
Raymond, thereby giving Lawrence a potential opportunity to get into the
game through Ken's initiating efforts. Ken's intention, however, is to promote Lawrence's independence from teacher negotiation. Van Hoorn and
her colleagues (1999) discuss such entry requests:

> Teachers may find that some children . . . have less experience, confi-
> dence or ability when engaging in play activities. Some consistently look
> to adults to help them enter the play of others. This is often true of chil-
> dren who are unable to communicate their needs clearly. (p. 95)

Ken's role with Lawrence will be to support interaction skills without in-
creasing his dependence on a teacher to facilitate such entry.

Matthew, unconcerned with Lawrence's challenge to the dyad, suggests a new theme for play. He dramatically throws his snack cup on the
climber platform, clearly against a school norm of cleanliness. "I'll just leave
this cup right *here*! Right? I'll just leave this cup right here, right?" Matthew
is upping the ante further, challenging the teacher's authority. He has
sought direct agreement from Raymond, twice prompting him with the

question "Right?" Matthew is attempting to secure a warrant from Raymond in the form of an acknowledgement, so that the episode can proceed. Children's use of such questions effectively continues the progression of the episode when new ideas are introduced. While Matthew has adopted the use of this question, prompting Raymond twice for confirmation, Matthew does not receive an acknowledgement from Raymond, who has been distracted by the return of Lawrence. Yelling, "Out! Out!", Raymond picks up Matthew's cup and throws it off the platform in the general area of Lawrence, who runs away.

Corsaro (1985, 1997) has found that evasion of adult rules enables children to gain a feeling of control over their lives. The act of challenge also secures affiliation among playmates. Sutton-Smith (1985) and Sutton-Smith and Byrne (1984) also write about naughty behavior in play, suggesting that the inversion of norms leads to greater social bonding and an outlet for emotions. In this case, Raymond and Matthew as players are developmentally just learning to establish a theme to their play. They are attracted to playing "naughty" because it offers a distinct integration in their otherwise disparate theme.

Upon Lawrence's retreat, Matthew and Raymond return to their original activity of performing impressive stunts for each other as they scramble up the metal slide. They have yet to sustain a mutual theme for their actions. As Matthew makes it to the top of the slide, Lawrence returns and attempts entry under the slide.

Matthew calls out in high-pitched alarm to Raymond, inviting him back to the top of the climber: "Hurry!" The running routine is evoked again, this time by Matthew. The theme change is established by both a verbal signal and a shift in voice register. It is prompted by the invasion of Lawrence, who has been thrust into the threatening role. Corsaro (1985) notes that threatening agents are often thrust into their role in a running routine.

Matthew continues, "Come in, let's get up! And let's go!" As Raymond and Lawrence struggle under the slide, Matthew slides down the slide and runs away.

Raymond calls out to him anxiously, "Matthew, I got him!"

Raymond and Lawrence separate and move out from under the slide. Matthew is long gone and probably does not even hear Raymond's call. Raymond and Lawrence both run away in the direction of Matthew. Matthew has fully enacted the running routine by leaving the area, prompting both Lawrence and Raymond to follow. Raymond catches up with Matthew. Lawrence runs by them both in the direction of the inside classroom.

As Lawrence passes them, Matthew turns to Raymond: "Come on, hurry! Chase Lawrence! That way." Running together, Raymond and

Matthew have cemented their interaction in a mutually recognized "chase Lawrence" theme.

ENACTMENT PHASE OF THE EPISODE

Raymond and Matthew return to the slide. Lawrence is close behind Raymond.

Raymond stops on the slide bottom to yell at Lawrence, "No, you're not allowed!"

Lawrence disagrees. "I . . . I will be allowed."

Raymond turns and follows Matthew up the slide.

Looking down at Lawrence, Matthew suggests, "All right, let's block it."

Raymond confirms Matthew's suggestion: "Yeah."

Raymond and Matthew use their bodies to block the entrance at the top of the slide. Now the play theme is thus explicitly defined and agreed upon as resisting entrance by another.

Lawrence moves away from the slide.

Raymond wraps himself around one of the main structure poles. "Look at . . . look at. Look at me!"

Matthew has lost interest. "What?"

"Look at me."

Quickly the chase/block theme is abandoned upon Lawrence's retreat. Matthew and Raymond return to performing stunts for each other. Matthew moves to sit on the top of the slide. The shared action is now characterized by a lack of intensity and a diffuse attention. Corsaro (1985) notes the necessity of "joint accomplishment" for this running away routine to be fully realized. Children play "with each other and for each other" (p. 237) as they chase back and forth together. Matthew and Raymond needed a third party to ignite an integrated theme. However, Lawrence is not comfortable in the role of intruder. The play theme is faltering without Lawrence's participation.

Lawrence has returned to Ken. He struggles to explain the problem he is having with Raymond at the slide. "I'm on the slide. Raymond tried . . . only . . . Raymond . . . Ken, I go on. Raymond slide down and *push* down."

"Tell him to leave you alone. Can you tell them that? When they come and bother you?"

Ken's intention here again is to promote Lawrence's ability to negotiate his interests independently from teacher aid. Ken suggests specific words for Lawrence to use when talking to Raymond.

Lawrence returns to the slide, calling out his request. "Raymond . . . I want to leave alone on the slide, O.K.?" Lawrence is rebuffed once more as Matthew and Raymond make a "block." As Lawrence retreats, Matthew cackles.

Raymond has found a stick on the platform. "Oh! Look at this *needle*! Look at needle—" Raymond's suggestion explicitly changes the theme of the interaction from associative play to the realm of pretend, though the hiding/running alliance is formed by the implicit fantasy that Lawrence is a "threat" when actually he is not.

As Raymond identifies the threatening needle, he moves close to Matthew and also hangs out over the platform in the direction of Lawrence. "I'll throw it at you, Lawr—"

Raymond has followed Matthew's sinister cackle with the initiation of a threat. In the context of the episode, Raymond's threat is his attempt to protect his alliance with Matthew from the intrusion of Lawrence. Corsaro (1985) documents the use of threats as a routine that emerges in episodes when children feel the need to protect their play interaction.

Raymond's retaliation only fuels Lawrence's complaints when he again returns to Ken. "He's have a needle and poke on my eye!"

Ken's reaction matches Lawrence's dramatic tone as he exclaims in incredulous astonishment: "Oh, no! I don't ever see these terrible things happen! Why do you suppose they're doing these terrible things to you, Lawrence?" Ken is here switching the focus of attention back to Lawrence's frame of reference.

Before Lawrence can appreciate the perspective of others, he needs first to understand his own perspective. Lawrence continues to detail Raymond's grievous behavior: "Raymond has a *needle* on him."

Ken is confused and slightly impatient. "He has what?"

"A needle."

Ken gently suggests with a note of tentativeness, "You need to find a place different to play from them, I think." Ken is respecting the integrity of Raymond's and Matthew's separate play event from the apparent intrusion of Lawrence. Ken is prompting Lawrence to make a decision as to whether he is actually interested in playing with Raymond and Matthew. Ken's suggestion of separation is also a paradoxical device. By suggesting a contrary alternative, Ken is hoping that Lawrence can more directly identify his own intentions and then act on this information. Clearly, Lawrence wants to play with Matthew and Raymond. Ken does not make any suggestions as to how to accomplish this goal.

Back at the climber, Matthew acknowledges Raymond's thematic transformation into the pretend. "Now I tryin' to find a needle."

Both Matthew and Raymond look on the ground for needles. Lawrence, having approached the climber, again returns to Ken for help. "Raymond has a needle to throw on my face."

Ken is still disbelieving. "He has a needle?" Ken is distracted and does not follow up on Lawrence's concern.

Matthew runs from the ground to the slide and ascends it as he hears Lawrence "telling." He is quite excited. "Oh, oh! He's telling!"

Raymond follows and they scramble up together. Matthew is adding another dimension to the play theme in his excitement to get away. The notion that needles are a source for threat is now accompanied by the implication that he and Raymond are doing something naughty.

Raymond responds to Matthew's enthusiasm with glee as he also runs up the slide. "Oh. Oh. Yea!"

Matthew and Raymond position themselves on the platform, waiting and watching for Ken and Lawrence. Matthew is beside himself with excitement, expressing himself in a higher tone than normal, and rather quickly. "Here, right here. H—here! It is a shot!" In his excitement, Matthew is adding further assault to the threatening needle by adding shooting powers.

Matthew calls out to Lawrence in traditional teasing singsong: "You aren't coming up here!"

Raymond moves next to Matthew.

Lawrence attempts another initiation into the dyad of Raymond and Matthew. "What y'are *making*?"

"So it'll block you."

"Is . . . a tunnel?" Lawrence suggests.

Raymond remains intent. "A block."

Lawrence tries to climb up, sees Raymond and Matthew as a block, and runs away.

Matthew cackles: "Good!"

Raymond rejoins. "Good. He's a doo-doo."

"Hey, two birdies . . . two birdies!" Matthew observes as he and Raymond stand on the platform.

Immediately upon the departure of Lawrence, the play theme returns from the transformed reality of needles and blocked entrances to the concrete world of birds in the yard.

Lawrence returns to Ken. "Raymond said no everybody on the—"

Ken interrupts Lawrence. He and Lawrence struggle to gain command. "You know wha', you know what, Lawrence?"

"—the slide."

"I think—you're gonna have to work this out yourself. Look. Listen, to me. Because every time you go over there, they're gonna say things to you. And you keep going over there, so I seem to think you *want* them to say these things to you. When you go over, they're gonna say things to you."

Ken attempts to show Lawrence his own role and consequential actions in the grievous interchange. During screening interviews, Ken acknowledged that he was never sure if children this young understood such an analysis. However, he felt it important to highlight individual participation in a play interaction that not only appeared repetitively problematic to him, but which was also coupled by complaints from a member of the interchange. As a problem solving strategy, Ken does not focus on the actions of a defined assailant. Rather, he turns attention back to Lawrence.

Lawrence is persistent. "But he's have a real needle and . . . throw on my eye."

"Whoa . . . he doesn't have a *real* needle. . . . You have lots of sand on you. Here. It probably feels like a needle, cuz it's sand. You O.K.?"

Lawrence relaxes. "My eyes have a lot of sand."

At this point Ken shifts to the initiation phase of interaction. "You want to play with them, Lawrence?"

"Nooo."

Ken is trying to clarify Lawrence's motives. The implication of Lawrence's negative response is that since he does not want to play with Matthew and Raymond, then he could refrain from going over to the slide area. It is unclear if Lawrence understands this important point or if he is ready to control his need for affiliation with his friend Raymond.

Matthew sees Lawrence talking to Ken and reinitiates the shared routine of running away. "Hurry . . . hurry!" They slide down the slide, then scramble back up.

Matthew shrieks in heightened excitement: "Hurry, but hurry! Up this way!" Matthew's tone of voice changes, and reflects the return of the feigned threat theme.

Raymond follows closely.

Matthew restates their possession of the slide, seeking Raymond's confirmation. "Be sure we get it, right?" While prompting Raymond, note that Matthew is linguistically unclear on the topic of his command. He may himself be unclear as to his reference.

Raymond nonetheless agrees. The interaction is comparatively tight and focused, with crisp back and forth verbal and nonverbal negotiations and use of register differences to repeatedly mark a vague but exciting retaliatory theme. Raymond, with an acorn, introduces a further retaliatory measure into the play theme: "Yeah . . . the one more time he comes up, throw this bullet at him. Kill him."

"Just two more bullets for me, all right?"

"All right."

Out of this sequence of focused questions and succinct agreement has come clear mutuality, which is the ingredient that fuels the elaboration of the theme. Matthew calls to Raymond to return to the platform. "Come on!"

Raymond climbs up the slide and delivers more bullets to Matthew, placing them in a pile on the platform. "I got you three."

Matthew marks Raymond's action with terse preparedness. "All right!" He counts up his collections from the upper deck. "I got two . . . I got two needles, and three bullets!"

Raymond comments from below as he searches the ground. "I'm gonna get . . . I'm gonna find more needles."

Matthew attempts to delimit the scope of Raymond's efforts. "Yeah, that's enough. For sure *eee*-nough."

"I'm gonna get more."

"You need two?"

"You do too."

Matthew attempts a limitation again. "Now, there," finally suggesting a change of location. "Now, let's go down."

"Oh, let's take the needles . . ." So integrated is the theme at this point that when Matthew suggests moving, Raymond facilitates the continuity of the theme by suggesting that they bring the play props with them.

Lawrence has been watching Matthew and Raymond from some distance. He returns to Ken for help.

"They have a needle, a needle to throw on my face."

"Let's ask 'em about this." Ken and Lawrence walk over to the large climber. Meanwhile, Raymond and Matthew are both off the slide structure and walking around the structure.

Raymond looks up. "Now, just—oh, there's Lawrence."

Matthew turns around and rushes back up the slide, with Raymond following. "No! He's . . . uh-oh, he's telling the teacher. He's telling the teacher! Down here!" Matthew jumps from the upper deck to the platform and begins frenetically jumping around in complete and delirious excitement.

Ken calls out to Raymond as he and Lawrence approach the climber. "Raymond?"

Matthew and Raymond are both running in circles around the second platform. "Oh, oh!"

Ken walks toward the structure and, looking up at Raymond, addresses the pretend context. "Raymond, could I see the needle that you keep talking about?" In asking Raymond in this way and by addressing the transformed theme without qualification or reference to reality, Ken maintains discourse at the pretend level. He also conveys credibility and acceptance of Raymond's perspective and actions.

Raymond readily shows Ken the needle as Ken moves up closer to the climber. Observing this interchange on tape, I was amazed at the facility with which Ken was able to proceed with a negotiation around discrepant perspectives. Earlier in the afternoon, another child had brought me out to the slide to negotiate a dispute with Raymond and Matthew. In that instance, coming in cold without any knowledge of the children's current play theme, and referring to the complaint from outside of any play theme, I was completely unsuccessful at eliciting Raymond's cooperation. In fact, my appearance only promoted further "naughty" activity, as both Matthew and Raymond refused to listen to me, covering their ears with their hands and running in a similarly frenetic fashion similar to that occasioned by Ken's appearance. Ken's ability to defuse this excitement, while at the same time acknowledging Raymond's and Matthew's perspective, is effective here in promoting negotiation.

Ken begins to structure a negotiation around the discrepancy in perspective between Lawrence and Raymond. "That's really scary. He really believes it's real, Lawrence does. I know it's pretend. But you need to tell him that, because he thinks it's real." Ken's personal acknowledgment of the pretend theme with the statement "I know it's pretend" has the effect of supporting Raymond's activity in pretend play. The statement also lets Raymond off the hook in the face of Lawrence's grievous complaints.

Raymond addresses Lawrence as directed. "Lawrence, the needle is just pretend."

Lawrence is within hearing, just next to the climber. He makes no visible sign that he has heard Raymond. Ken prompts a response from Lawrence. "Did you hear that, Lawrence?"

Without any pause, Lawrence quickly responds forcefully, "No!"

Ken structures the negotiation further, and asks Raymond, "Say it again."

Raymond complies, calling out even more loudly to Lawrence. "*Lawrence!* The needle is just pretend."

Lawrence looks up to Raymond and gazes steadily into his face from below.

Ken pauses for a moment, waiting for Lawrence to speak. As Lawrence continues to gaze upwards at Raymond, Ken prompts again. "Did you hear it that time, Lawrence?"

Lawrence persists in feeling threatened from the play theme. "But is all the needles can flying away." Lawrence's acquisition of English as a second language shows in his distress.

Ken calmly and slowly reassures Lawrence in a low tone. "He says it's *pretend*." Ken pauses. "It's not really real."

Ken then turns his attention to Raymond and Matthew, making explicit what he believes to be an unstated motive in this triadic interaction. He is very careful and slightly tentative here in his suggestion. "You know what, you guys? Lawrence . . . Lawrence, I think wants to play with you."

Raymond quickly rejects the idea: "No!"

Ken repeats Raymond's intentions. "No, you don't want him to play with you?" Ken is slowing the pace of this negotiation in order that all three players are aware of this significant piece of information.

Raymond repeats his intention. "No."

Matthew is also shaking his head "no."

Ken continues. "Well, you need to—you need to *tell* him that, 'cause he d—, I think he's getting confused, 'cause sometimes he thinks you're playing with him and he's not . . . he's not sure."

Raymond and Matthew are arranging their collection of needles and bullets as Ken says this. Ken slowly moves away, having accepted Raymond's and Matthew's decision to play by themselves. Lawrence moves away also. Ken's strategy in this sequence is to make explicit the intentions of Raymond and Matthew. In fact, Ken may be forcing an explicit statement from Matthew and Raymond in order to halt the recurrent approach and flee actions between Lawrence, Raymond, and Matthew. Ken seeks out Lawrence at the sand kitchen where he is stirring sand in a bowl.

Ken offers Lawrence a sandy cup. "Would you like a little bit of lemonade, Lawrence? Mmm! Mmm, mm. What have you got here? This is a different kind of . . . is that . . . ? Is that your pie and lemonade?"

"No."

Ken probes further. "No? What is it?"

Lawrence responds, struggling for the appropriate word in English. "It's my . . . Ap . . ."

Ken suggests a possibility. "Apple crisp?"

Lawrence extends Ken's suggestion. "Apple pie and . . . it's . . . it's my ap, ap, . . . apple strudel."

Ken acknowledges Lawrence's transformation. "Apple strudel, yum, yum."

Meanwhile, Matthew and Raymond shift to a game of sliding acorns down the slide. The theme drops once again from pretend to being reality-based. The episode ends after a fourth player attempts initiation and is rejected, and Matthew and Raymond again try out stunts for each other.

REVIEW OF THE EPISODE

Sociodramatic play is elusive for Raymond and Matthew in this episode. The two boys are beginning players who find opportunities in the ecology of the large climber to test out their burgeoning feelings of power and control. Raymond is not intent on hurting Lawrence physically, as he refrains from actually kicking or hitting him, but rather protects his interaction with Matthew, which is tenuous at best. As anyone in play yard confrontations can remember, however, such confrontation can be psychologically stunning even when the intention is to protect a fragile alliance. Both Raymond and Matthew challenge Ken's expectations for cleanliness and safety as, with unbridled enthusiasm and mock terror, they launch Ken into the nonnegotiated role of threat. Raymond and Matthew never do assign or define roles for themselves in their game, making elaboration of their "Hurry, let's hide" game difficult. Due to the flexibility of cues for play in the large climber ecology, Raymond and Matthew are ready to attach a threatening role to a third party but need practice in imagining who they themselves might be. Challenges to friendship allegiances also surface in the ecology from the physical features of the large climber. Entry points can be accessed or blocked at will. Teachers will find that any ecology that includes entry points offers the opportunity to control access.

The episode is marked by ritualized and repetitive behavior at the climber as Lawrence attempts initiation and is rebuffed numerous times. Ritualized repetitive behavior often emerges when language is unavailable, as it is for Lawrence, who is using English as his second language. Lawrence is more at ease engaging in sociodramatic play in the more explicit ecology of the sand kitchen. Sand kitchen routines are more familiar and Ken's language and social skills offer Lawrence practice while in the comfort of Ken's adult competency. Ken is also not threatening to put out his eye with a needle and kill him with acorn bullets.

Mead (1934) would say that Raymond and Matthew are in the first of three stages in the development of the self, the play stage. After initial rejection of Lawrence to protect play with each other, Raymond and Matthew evolve the exclusion further. They incite Lawrence in their repeated attempts to create a response to their "naughty" actions. Mead would argue that Raymond and Matthew, in adopting a naughty theme to their play, are beginning individually to make sense of how others view them. Raymond and Matthew are being naughty to get Lawrence to complain to Ken so they can rebel against Ken's adult authority. Being "naughty" allows them to make sense of classroom expectations for appropriate behavior.

The episode is marked by a number of sophisticated features. Raymond and Matthew collect make-believe needles and bullets. Raymond uses a verbal suggestion of make-believe with his plan: "One more time he comes up here, throw this bullet at him. Kill him." There is verbal interaction to clarify and negotiate: Raymond and Matthew are not making a tunnel for entry, as Lawrence hopes; they are making a block, to exclude. There is practice in the skills of numeration and classification: Raymond sorts and collects needles and bullets. Matthew attempts a delimiter on the collection as Raymond tallies the balance of artillery that each has. Ken facilitates the distinction between reality and fantasy for Lawrence and encourages perspective-taking, saying to Matthew and Raymond "That's really scary. He really believes it's real, Lawrence does. I know it's pretend. But you need to tell him that, because he thinks it's real."

Probably the most visible complexity in this episode involves the constant challenge for attention. As young social partners, Raymond and Matthew need to work hard to keep each other's attention. Early on, Raymond suggests a "look at me" game, familiar as a family repertoire, but one with little room to develop into a theme with peers. The game is superseded by the far more potent "feigned fear," which cements Raymond and Matthew in mutual play. As the element of threat is removed, the episode ends in a return to "look at me."

The other side of "feigned fear" is the attempt to induce real fear in Lawrence. This aspect of ganging up on the "it" person in the run-and-hide games is given scant attention in the literature. Ken acknowledges Lawrence's fear, explaining that he thinks the game is real, not pretend. The dynamic, nonetheless, is real, as in many "feigned fear" situations. Part of the dynamic is to have a play group create an enemy by "feigning fear" and then, like scientists investigating how emotions can be triggered, create real fear in the identified other. This stage of development can be characterized as gaining individuation, attention, and acceptance by the peer group; doing so, however, at the expense of the one singled out. Gallas (1998) offers insight, noticing that mean-spirited "bad-boy" behavior is a role some children adopt when in the company of others in the classroom. These children are "on stage," so to speak, and act very different in private interactions. It is the possibility of attention that creates an irresistible role for these children:

> Children's social actions are almost always within their control. If they are threatening or intimidating others, I believe they know what they are doing. I also believe that they are hoping for an honest response from everyone present because they are trying on ways of being in the world. The classroom, the playground, and the neighborhood are like experimental test sites for later life. Everyone needs to know the positive and negative effects of what they do. Bad boys, like most children, are not naturally mean spirited; they are experimental. They are small social

scientists studying the effects of their behavior on others. . . . They need thoughtful "others" helping them to reflect upon and take responsibility for their actions. (pp. 43–44)

As teachers in the yard, we offer children a means mutually to reflect on the intentions of their experimentations.

Ken adopts a number of strategies throughout the episode. For most of the episode Ken is an *observer*, reflecting on his observations with Lawrence and building a hypothesis with Lawrence about his repeated efforts to enter play. The teacher-observer strategy is discussed by Van Hoorn and her colleagues (1999), Reynolds and Jones (1997) and Trawick-Smith (1994) as a teacher tool for appreciating the perspective of children during play. Ken extends his observations to the triad as well, which serves a mediating function. The peacemaker role is described by Van Hoorn and her colleagues (1999) to account for strategies that help mediate conflicts by either suggesting alternative roles that stretch children's thinking beyond the dispute in question, or interpreting playmate motives or behavior. As a *peacemaker*, Ken initially helps clarify Lawrence's interest in entry into play, and later makes the pretend aspect of Raymond and Matthew's game explicit for Lawrence's psychological safety. Van Hoorn and her colleagues (1999) also identify a "guardian of the gate" role for teachers. A *guardian of the gate* both protects children's interactive play and supports children's developing skills in play entry. In this episode, Ken accepts Raymond's choice to play exclusively with Matthew and offers himself as a *player* when Lawrence chooses the sand kitchen ecology. As a player, Ken suggests ideas, modeling play props in a pretend mode and facilitates conversational flow while allowing Lawrence to direct the pace and action of the interaction. Enhancing sociodramatic play with Lawrence, Ken adopts the role of *play tutor* (Smilansky, 1968; Trawick-Smith, 1994), using a sandy cup as lemonade and suggesting that Lawrence's sand concoction might be pie. Trawick-Smith suggests that such play intervention is especially helpful to ease anxieties of children who are confused about fantasy and reality, though he recommends subtle intervention into the threatening theme itself, which Ken does not do. From Ken's perspective, Matthew and Raymond have an intact interaction, which does not need assistance. From Ken's perspective, the best way to alleviate Lawrence's anxiety would be for him to stop participating in the interaction.

Lawrence is perhaps as confused by his friend Raymond's excluding him as he is by the threatening theme. While Lawrence plays comfortably with Raymond out of school when adults have arranged the play date, in a group setting Lawrence is less sure of his independent skills in gaining entry. Teachers adopting the role of *guardian of the gate* can suggest additional roles for a child seeking entry. In this episode, however, Raymond and Matthew are just barely able to adopt their own roles independent of an external source, and are not communicatively ready to negotiate with a third player as ally. Karen offers another alternative to Lawrence in the next episode, where her setup arrangement allows parallel play among children. Lawrence will have the opportunity to practice entry skills and watch accomplished peer players interact.

3   Making a New Road

Credit: Lynn Bradley

THE PLAY STRATEGIES children use when they pretend are high-lighted in this episode involving three children who are regular play partners. Both Karen's setup arrangement and the children's own mastered interaction skills allow the episode to progress generally independent of Karen's involvement. The episode nicely shows how the children's play is framed and influenced by Karen's setup of the sand pit.

On this particular day, Karen's setup for the sand pit involves separating the ecology into two symmetrical areas for group interaction. She places two large trucks at each end of the sand pit. She returns with four large shovels, placing two shovels at each end with the trucks. She lays a large, flat wooden cover from a toy chest as a bridge between the two play spaces. Her setup is a geometrical configuration, which has created two separate play spaces suggesting digging and construction. Each play space suggests a spot for two players. With the placement of the wooden cover, she suggests the possibility for interaction between the two spaces if children are ready for the more complex challenge of interacting in a larger group. Karen's symmetrical arrangement creates an opportunity for an onlooker or parallel player to move into interactive play. This arrangement is particularly supportive to children whose skills in initiation are not securely developed. A child can conceivably claim a truck in a space opposite from one where children are interacting and drive across the bridge to participate. The bridge acts as both a literal and figurative entry point for play initiation.

The resulting episode elegantly exemplifies Karen's intentions for sufficient spatial boundaries, as established by her setup cues. As Lawrence plays at one side of the ecology, Danny and Seth move in to occupy the adjacent space at the other end of the sand pit. The sand pit is large enough that, adjacent to Lawrence, another group will play independently throughout the entire length of the episode. Karen's setup clearly provides separate and sufficient space for comfortable play with small groups.

The episode begins just 10 minutes before the class will meet inside for a large group circle. Karen is occupied with restoration of the yard, including sweeping and the shelving of toys not currently in use. She monitors the yard's activities as she works. While Karen is not a featured interactant in the episode, the effect of her setup is striking. The children themselves use spatial management to maintain the interaction. In the section "Review of the Episode" at the end of this chapter, I will more directly address Karen's role as teacher.

Participants in this episode include the three regular playmates, Danny, age 4 years, 11 months; Seth, age 5 years, 2 months; Chris, age 5 years, 2 months; and Lawrence, age 4 years, 6 months. This play episode lasts 13 minutes.

INITIATION AND NEGOTIATION PHASES OF THE EPISODE

The episode begins with the entrance of Danny into an unoccupied space at one end of the sand pit, just past Lawrence, who is playing with a dump truck. Danny is carrying a large dump truck. He accompanies his arrival with musical emphasis: "Da da dum!" His use of musical accompaniment here signals his initiation into the realm of pretend play, where actions have a dramatic significance beyond their concrete physical expression. The musical accompaniment is a cue, which marks the event as pretend. Danny positions himself at one end of the sand pit.

Seth follows, bringing two small cars. "Look what I got! Two of these trucks." Seth sits and drives both cars side by side in the sand, having renamed his cars "trucks" to align himself with Danny.

Danny stands over Seth, and sets up the first rule for their play. "You have to share one."

"O.K. . . . I'll share with you." Seth throws one of the cars to Danny, saying, "This one."

"O.K., that one's for me." Seth and Danny are already negotiating what props to use to identify a theme to their mutual play. The fact that both Danny and Seth are carrying toy vehicles indicates that the initiation of the episode has occurred prior to their entry into the ecology. With regular play partners, such initiation often occurs quickly and in shorthand, a more distinct example of which will be seen in the next chapter. In this episode, Danny and Seth seek out the sand pit ecology as their place to play. The verbal marker "O.K." is used by both playmates to acknowledge their mutuality. Such tight interactive acknowledgment is one feature of accomplished players.

Seth jumps up to get another vehicle, clutching his first car tightly to his chest. "I'll get the Chevy!"

He returns with a large jeep and sits down next to Danny, announcing the accomplishment of his task. "I got my Chevy . . ." Seth's comment grounds the play action, making the progress of play clearer. Seth also establishes the play theme here. They are playing Chevies. He includes Danny in the fantasy. "I . . . you already have a Chevy!"

Danny accepts the idea and the theme is explicitly negotiated. "All right." The manner of theme negotiation is tied specifically and concretely to props.

Danny pushes his car, making engine sounds. "Mmmmm."

Seth picks up a similarly sized car and runs it side by side with Danny. "Rrrrrrrrr." With the cars as explicit props, Seth and Danny have negotiated an agreed play theme and commence the enactment of the theme. Chris arrives and squats in the sand with his toy garden hoe, watching. Lawrence remains in solitary play with his dump truck in the middle of the ecology.

ENACTMENT PHASE OF THE EPISODE

Danny calls out to his friend in the car. "Hi, buddy!" With this address, Danny elaborates a role for himself and Seth in the driving theme.

Seth responds as a driver, thereby recognizing the new role. "Hi!" The enactment phase proceeds between these two players-as-drivers.

"How are you doing?" Danny calls out.

"Fine," says Seth, as he and Danny drive next to Lawrence.

Chris waves his hoe. "Here, anybody want this?" he says, attempting an initiation into the play.

Danny declines and swings his car in a wide curve around Chris. "No thanks. Eouuu . . ."

Seth, aware of Chris's interest in being included, follows Danny, securing his alliance with the suggestion, "This a twin." Typical of many triadic play groups, Seth's subtle jockeying for attention from Danny will continue throughout the episode.

Lawrence follows Danny, making his own entry attempt into the interaction. "Watch this! Watch this! Neh . . . Neh. . . ." Lawrence moves his dump truck along the same path taken by Danny.

Danny looks back at Lawrence momentarily, then drives over to join Seth.

Seth addresses Danny. "Look what I got—"

Chris is still holding the hand hoe. "I got the hoe!" He follows Danny, suggesting a partnership, with his hoe. "Let's say . . . let's say these were buddies." He uses the same referent Danny used to acknowledge the pretend theme with Seth. Chris begins to dig a road with his hoe.

Danny turns to watch, then begins driving on Chris's road. "Hi, buddy!" With Danny's acceptance of Chris as "buddy," Chris is now included in the driver game.

Chris elaborates on the theme. "You need a crash road?"

Lawrence stands up and walks over to Chris and Danny, attempting to enter the play. "You . . . ," he says quietly and with some hesitancy.

Danny responds quickly. "Oh, no, I'd like a new road, that's what I'd like!"

Chris takes Danny up on his suggestion and begins to make a road in front of Danny's car. With Chris hoeing and Danny following behind, a subtle alliance has been established between Chris and Danny in a mutual chase routine.

Lawrence squats down directly in front of Chris, moving in quite close to Chris's face. He attempts another initiation. "You's making a new road, right?" Danny's explicit verbalization opens up an avenue for Lawrence's interactive exchange.

Danny stretches to get his face close and between Chris and Lawrence. He faces Lawrence. "*I* want a new road, get it, not you, too." Danny turns back to driving his car, not wanting to be distracted in his alliance with Chris.

The noted Swiss psychologist Jean Piaget (1962, 1969) believed that development and learning occur through a constructive process guided by the child's initiative. After extensive observation of the developmental stages of play in young children, Piaget concluded that group fantasy play offers opportunities for conflicts in roles and rules for peer play. Conflicts such as negotiating multiple playmate perspectives and negotiating between reality and fantasy become cognitive and social challenges that further intellectual development. Danny, Chris, Seth, and Lawrence will continue to negotiate play perspectives throughout this episode.

Lawrence repeats his last attempt at initiation into the game: "You making a new road?"

Seth moves up next to Danny. "He said, 'You making a poo poo road?'" Seth's rebuff, coming as it does with Danny and Chris having secured an allegiance as a dyad, is a way both to exclude the addition of another competing player and to realign himself with Danny, his original play partner.

Lawrence stands up and walks away from the others, moving toward the dump truck. "No!" he says quickly. He begins to move the dump truck. "I'm making a poo poo—"

Seth begins a series of announcements about his jeep as Danny and Chris continue on the new road.

"This guy is going up the hill."

"This guy is dumping his truck out."

Seth finds a smaller car like Danny's, driving the car back to Danny and Chris. "Duuhm! Dah dum!"

Seth is trying hard to provide something interesting and attractive enough to warrant his acceptance into the play between Danny and Chris. At this point in the episode Seth is the odd man out, though he started out as Danny's play partner. Chris's elegant suggestion of making a new road has altered Danny's and Seth's game and left Seth out of the loop. Lawrence, being a less experienced player, is similarly rebuffed, though not rejected as in the prior episode with Raymond and Matthew.

Seth drives his car over the road used by Danny. Danny moves his truck next to Seth's, offering Seth an invitation into the game: "Oooonly little trucks allooooowed." Danny then drives in a fast-paced trip along the curves of the road to Chris. "Is this, is this da end of da road?" Danny is signaling Chris's dominance here in adopting a baby voice, coincident with his invitation of Seth into an elaboration of the game, a new road extension.

"Yep. Have to make it some more, now," Chris responds.

Seth moves his car next to Danny's. Chris extends the road. Seth and Danny begin laughing as they try to catch up to Chris. With Danny's assurance of Chris's leadership, Seth is accepted into the game through the routine of chasing. Chasing, as will be discussed in the final chapter, is a powerful game in the peer group. It functions to solidify acceptance and partnership. While moving small cars around a confined area does not connote a "chase" in the technical sense, the dynamic of one playmate in front with others following is the same.

While Chris marks a road with his hoe, Danny and Seth begin crawling frantically behind, driving their two cars and laughing in clearly acknowledged mutuality.

Chris stops the hoe emphatically, digging it into the sand briefly to mark the end of the road. "Stop!" Danny and Seth drive into the mark in the sand, piling up.

Danny politely marks the end of this action. "Thanks a lot."

Danny then turns to Seth and laughs again.

Chris looks up and notices the video camera. "The movie camera," he remarks casually. It is interesting at this point of alliance between Seth and Danny that Chris finds a situation for interruption.

"The movie camera?" asks Danny. He looks up, sees the camera, and quickly scrambles up and abandons the play site. As he runs, Danny is looking back at the camera. Chris and Seth follow, dropping their toys and keeping their eyes fixed on Danny. Danny stops mid-yard. The three gather together outside the sand pit, looking to each other. Danny notices that the camera appears to be pointing away from their play spot. Danny returns to the sand, with Chris and Seth following. All three scramble for their abandoned toys.

Lawrence wants to go on the road.

Chris offers to make a road for him. "I'll make you a new one, O.K.?"

Danny agrees. "Yeah. Make him a big one for him." Danny's suggestion is an interesting reflection of Karen's setup. With his suggestion he shows he is aware of the necessity of careful spatial arrangements when playing with multiple partners and needs during play.

Danny jumps up and runs over to Chris as Lawrence says: "You make . . . make . . . so can drive—"

Interrupting Lawrence, Danny begins to drive along the road Chris is making for Lawrence. "Brrrrr!"

"—Rocka Canyon Road Circle. You, you make, uhm, this drive," continues Lawrence to Chris.

Chris has now finished making Lawrence's road. "O.K.! Lawrence? Your road," directs Chris. He is smoothing the road over. "O.K.?"

"'Kay," Lawrence says immediately.

Chris repeats his directions with soft reassurance. "See, this is *your* road." He smoothes out the road gently. "O.K.?" Chris supports Lawrence's understanding of the play context with simple, direct, and concrete directions.

Lawrence responds to Chris's prompting with a repetition of the directive. "This is *my* road."

Danny, who has been watching Chris's actions, reinforces this new addition to the play episode. "Yeah, it's your road." Danny's comment, though obvious, functions as repetition, making clear the elaboration of the game to include a second road for Lawrence as a parallel player. Danny and Chris have elegantly met Lawrence's need to gain play experience. They offer themselves as mentors for Lawrence to watch.

What follows is a jostling of position in the boys' attempt to continue the driving game. Just as during other points of transition in this episode, an appeal to props is made, and all three scramble for more toys from the adjacent shelf.

Seth and Danny have trucks, and Chris has a long, heavy cardboard tube. Chris identifies his prop. "I got a little steamroller." The episode is in transition now as the old theme appears abandoned and a new one is yet to be negotiated.

The writings of Soviet psychologist Lev Vygotsky (1967, 1978) reinforce the experience that Karen, observing this play, understands well: children use play props to "anchor" pretend play until symbolic capabilities have developed. Ecologies therefore place differing demands on the child's capacity for representational thought, depending on the explicitness of area cues and props. The cardboard tube will challenge Danny and the others to elaborate on a new theme.

Danny pauses to look at Chris's roller. He marks the addition of a new thematic prop, "We . . . have to share tha-at."

Chris is rolling the tube lengthwise in the sand. He lifts it up and sets it vertically, suggesting it be an explosive. "Know what? But this is gonna be a cap."

Not having received confirmation, Danny tries again, at the same time elaborating, "We could share that and put sand in there."

"Yeah, r'ember dat time we did it?" Chris adds in a deferential baby voice.

"Oh, yeah," agrees Danny. With Chris's agreement to share, the two cement the transformation to a new game within the same episode. The theme is incorporated into the episode with a reference to a past and shared play event in the ecology. Theme development is concretely tied to props. The shift in theme is marked by Chris's change of register into a subtle baby voice where lowering his status is coincident with Danny's acceptance of the elaboration of the theme.

Lawrence turns from where he has been playing with the dump truck, and addresses Chris from the prior play theme. "Chris, you want to make a new road?"

Chris answers emphatically, "No!" Lawrence's intentions here are to practice entry into play, since his road is still relatively intact.

Danny also comments dramatically and in mock incredulousness: "A new road, *again*?!"

Chris now announces a new play rule. "No, Lawrence. You wrecked it, you make it."

Danny confirms Chris's remarks. "Yeah, you wrecked it, you make it." Without pause, however, Danny quickly decides to comply with Lawrence's appeal. "O.K., I'll make one for you." Danny begins using a large shovel to further mark out a road for Lawrence. He is making the road away from where he and Chris are playing with the cardboard tube. Once again, the intentions of Karen's setup are interestingly reflected in the children's independent negotiating of a separate but adjacent play space. Karen prepared the ecology for separate but adjacent play, which Danny has offered as an option for Lawrence.

Delighted with this effort, Lawrence laughs happily. "You make one for mine, right?"

"Yeah."

Lawrence moves his dump truck onto his road, driving it down an incline in the sand. "This is so wide, it makes go down hill, up hill, and down, down, and up hill, and . . ." Lawrence drives his truck into the opposite end of the sand pit where another group is playing. Just when Lawrence has a chance to engage in his own play theme, he chooses to abandon his play space in order to practice initiating with a new group of players.

Children from the other group call out in irritation: *"Don't! Don't!"*

Karen has been watching from a distance until rising voices signal her. She comes over and addresses Lawrence's immediate actions. "Don't drive your truck into those kids, please." During the tape screening, Karen commented that she wanted to stop Lawrence's action without threatening his continued participation in the area of play. As a child who has difficulty sustaining play with others, this play event is somewhat unique. Karen wanted to promote Lawrence's participation as much as possible by addressing a single action without disrupting the continuity of his interactions.

Danny begins to fill the tube with sand.

Lawrence, having accepted Karen's directive and returning to the original play group, approaches Danny. "What's *this* inside? What's *this* inside?" He moves closer to the tube again, watching as Danny fills the tube with sand. Lawrence is savvy enough to know the sand is representing something else in the game.

Danny is getting frustrated as the tube tips. "*Sand* is *inside!*" While Danny has adopted an explosive theme, he is not yet comfortable revealing it to Lawrence.

Chris makes the play theme explicit. "And it's called a firecracker!"

Lawrence holds the tube to look down into it.

"Don't!" yells Chris.

Lawrence jumps back. He turns slightly and moves away a little.

Danny continues to chastise Lawrence, then offers a possible negotiated settlement. "Lawrence, ahhh. Lawrence! . . . Guess you just want to *watch* us."

Lawrence accepts an onlooker position and sits down next to the firecracker. "'Kay."

Chris, however, is more demonstrative. "You can only watch us, O.K.?"

"Yeah!"

As noted by Corsaro (1985), children do appear to negotiate for space and membership based on some awareness of an upper limit to what can be successfully managed in the play episode. The "Making a New Road" episode suggests further that children also negotiate the maintenance of the play episode based on accumulated knowledge of the different styles of playmates. While Danny and Chris are unwilling to include Lawrence directly, they are more than willing to accommodate him as an adjacent, observing player. Their earlier reprimand, "You wrecked it, you make it," in this context can be interpreted as an attempt to instruct Lawrence in skills in enacting the play theme.

Lawrence moves to the base of the firecracker with his dump truck. "Errrr!"

Chris is concerned that Lawrence is about to wreck the firecracker setup. "No! No! Lawrence, no!" he yells out in a menacing, loud, anxious, and rising tone.

Lawrence moves away slightly and continues to drive his dump truck. "Errr!"

Chris is much calmer now. "No, that way, O.K.? Don't come this way."

"Errrr!" continues Lawrence.

Danny continues to fill the firecracker. He smoothes the sand from the top of the firecracker. "Oh. Almost to da top. Almost to da top." Danny adopts a baby voice as he marks progress in Chris's game.

Chris jumps with excitement. He and Danny push the firecracker over. "*Now*. It's a firecracker!"

"Poooooom!" Danny makes the sound of a firecracker explosion.

Seth watches as Danny and Chris tip over the firecracker. They quickly retrieve the tube and begin filling again.

Seth begins to comment as he moves his car in a long curve around the firecracker area. "This guy's going on the road. This guy's making a road. Down, down!" Seth gets close to the firecracker.

Chris warns him, "Don't! Firecracker!"

Danny follows Chris's lead and announces authoritatively, "Firecracker near you!"

Seth stands up and looks into the firecracker. As he moves away, he accidentally knocks the firecracker down.

Danny calls out accusingly in an adult tone of reprimand, "Seth!"

Chris follows Danny's accusatory tone, "Seeeth!"

Danny begins to shovel sand again. "'Kay, want me to put the next bunch of sand in?"

The firecracker tips over again, this time because it is not held firmly in the sand. Seth is not even close to the firecracker. Danny is getting really frustrated. "*Seth. Don't* help us."

Seth moves in and stands in front of Danny. Seth is annoyed and struggles to express his feelings of injustice. "Nope—heeeey! Who's—I can help yoooou!"

The firecracker falls a third time as Danny tries to fill it. Danny begins to think that perhaps Seth can, in fact, help. "Yeah, him can, you see?"

Chris will accept Seth into the play only conditionally, assigning Seth the role of helping him to wedge the bottom of the firecracker deep into the sand. "O.K. Only if he *helps* me. Through in *this* too harder . . . place."

Danny and Chris have agreed to let Seth participate. Danny again confirms the arrangements for Seth's involvement. "Yeah. Can he . . . can he only help you do that part and I put in the sand?"

"Yeah."

Seth's participating role is now established by the two original firecracker players. The negotiation is aided by the concrete designation of specific roles within the play interaction, either pouring sand or holding the firecracker. The episode ends with a final jockeying for position as Seth helps to fill the firecracker before everyone is interrupted by the call for inside group time.

REVIEW OF THE EPISODE

This sociodramatic play episode offers an opportunity to study the interaction strategies used by three children quite familiar and successful at playing together. The episode is a good example of practices for successful peer play that Danny, Seth, and Chris have developed over the course of a shared history. The episode also involves attempts to play by a fourth child, and the consequent adjustments made by the threesome to accommodate Lawrence in the play space. The children's leap into pretend play is specifically associated with available props in the ecology. Danny, Seth, and Chris all rely on thematically cued toys to suggest and barter for an agreed-upon theme. Ensuing negotiations involve not only the toy's features and functions but also include Danny's requirement for sharing, which emphasizes the mutuality of any progress.

The episode is marked by the typical jockeying for loyalties that often occur during triadic play where two players in effect trade allegiances with the third. In this case, Danny and Seth begin a driving game, which elaborates into a driving on Chris's road game. "Buddy" is used as a shorthand that marks allegiance. "This 'a twin'" reinforces player bond. The chase routine surfaces at the completion of the road game, marking both the fragility of the episode at that point of transition and Chris's need for reassurance of his inclusion. Loyalties are again challenged with Lawrence's interest in making a new road, and Danny and Chris settle on an elegant solution whereby Lawrence can watch in an adjacent space. Danny and Chris develop an ensuing firecracker game to which Seth seeks repeated entrance. In the next episode, Ken will also juggle multiple allegiances as children struggle to negotiate differing interests in the same ecology.

This episode involves direct and explicit signals of fantasy with specific negotiating phrases such as "pretend that . . ." and "let's say . . ." which not only signal "this is pretend" but at the same time initiate new ideas. Other occasions where signals for pretend were used, such as musical accompaniment, sounds, shifts in voice tone, and the use of commentary function to pack the episode richly with cues. Multiple cues ensure player awareness of the episode's action and topic. Warrants, those cues for permission to initiate or elaborate on a theme, are regularly secured to acknowledge theme recognition, usually with the add-on phrase "O.K.?" A shift in register to a baby voice is used to signal deference during negotiations as an effort to facilitate the proceedings, twice marking a shift in theme and once marking the theme's progress after elaboration.

The episode's pretend content marks its sophistication. Danny and Seth describe pretend driving action in commentary. Danny and Chris orchestrate an elaborate clarification of play space territory for Lawrence. They recognize his interest in the play theme and negotiate a solution that will account for his perspective while maintaining their own separate play group. A cardboard tube is substituted for a firecracker and roles are negotiated to facilitate involvement from all three players as well as onlooker involvement from Lawrence.

Karen's most prominent orchestration strategy is her *organization of the environment*, noted by Jones and Reynolds (1992), Trawick-Smith (1994), and Van Hoorn and her colleagues (1999). Based on her setup arrangements of play props, the ecology can accommodate three play configurations: Danny, Chris and Seth, Lawrence, and an adjacent group on the periphery. So evident is her spatial strategy of establishing separate but adjacent play spots in the ecology that Danny and Chris use it themselves to protect their interaction and thereby extend the episode when Lawrence desires entry into the triadic play. Throughout the episode, Karen functions as an *observer*, entering only at a point where Lawrence may be compromising his participation. She *mediates* the dispute between Lawrence and the second play group in such a way that Lawrence remains involved in interaction at the sand pit, while *protecting* the interactive space of the second group. Throughout the episode, she *restores* play areas to promote ongoing play for the following day. During the course of the episode, under Karen's direction from setup alone, problem solving occurs over the needs of multiple players. Creativity and flexible thinking are apparent as Danny and Chris numerically manage placement and roles, toys, and shared space in the ecology. Refined skills in impulse control occur despite excitement and frustration. In the next episode, children will manage similar challenges in the company of Ken-as-player.

4   *"The Dam Is Breaking!"*

Credit: Lynn Bradley

THIS EPISODE also occurs in the sand pit ecology. Suggestions for play are established directly from Ken's initial setup. Ken digs a center mound of sand and surrounds it with a four-sided trench. He sticks two shovels halfway up the mound on one side and places a road construction truck midway up the mound, leaving a marked, flat path where he has run the truck. Ken also snips three holes in an old truck tire tube and places the tube at one end of the sand pit. He fits one end of a hose into the tube so that when he turns the water on, three separate areas across the surface of the tire tube spout water.

The ensuing small group pretend play episode is representative of those occurring under Ken's direction. Ken moves in and out of the play episode, involving himself variously as observer and player within the event. One of the players, Casey, has just returned to school after a long absence due to surgery. He and Ken share a close relationship both in and out of school. Casey is somewhat anxious upon this first day back, and keeps a close tie to Ken throughout the episode.

Theme progression in this episode is influenced both by standard expectations for a sand play area, such as digging and water channeling, and by expectations derived from personally shared past experiences of play between Ken and many of the participating players. Such past experience would suggest that whatever occurs in the sand pit probably will involve expressions of heightened drama by Ken, as well as Ken's involvement as a player.

This episode also clearly documents the process of negotiation of different player intentions as the episode progresses. Players involved in the episode include Lawrence, age 4 years, 6 months; Raymond, age 4 years, 4 months; Robert, age 4 years, 11 months; Casey, age 4 years, 6 months; and Dora, age 5 years, 2 months. The full episode lasted 55 minutes, 23 minutes of which are highlighted here.

INITIATION PHASE OF THE EPISODE

Lawrence and Raymond have been mixing and digging sand and water. Ken sits adjacent to the play area, watching. Robert is next to Ken and is also watching. A rhythmic singsong between Robert, Raymond, and Lawrence develops concerning the mud forming around the water spouts.

"Goody mud butt."
"Goody mud butt."
"Goody mud water."
"Goody mud water."
"Goody mud water, we can have a whole stream!"
"Goody mud water, can have a whole stream."
"Goody mud water."
"Dirty mud here."
"Goody mud smooch. Goody smooch mud. Goody smooch mud."
"Goody smooch mud."

Raymond laughs. The rhythmic singsong has been identified by Opie and Opie (1959) as "tangletalk." Tangletalk is an intentional "juxtaposition of incongruities" in children's songs and rhymes. Gallas (1998) documents it as a form of intimate exchange among affiliated play parties. Corsaro (1986) identifies such rhythmic singsong as a routine within the peer culture which functions to integrate players in a shared activity. Here, this rhythmic exchange ties Robert, Raymond, and Lawrence together as players with the inclusive "we can have a whole stream."

NEGOTIATION PHASE OF THE EPISODE

Lawrence stands up and begins to move around the stream. "Rrrrr . . . Rrrrrr. I'm over the river now . . . Over the river," he says in an engine voice.

Casey now enters the sand pit. "Hi, Ken!"

"Hi, Casey," says Ken. Casey begins to finger a hole in the spouting tire, stopping the water.

"Stop! You're making it so I can't make it go down the stream!" Robert yells. "Tell him what you're doing, Robert," Ken says, prompting Robert to make his play intentions explicit.

"So, so the stream can't even move!" says Robert.

"But I think we have to wait, so it will go even faster," adds Casey.

"*Right*. So let's make a dam!" invites Robert.

"Yeah!" agrees Casey. With Ken's prompting, Robert has explained his plan for play. Once verbalized, Casey's information provides an opening for Casey to enter as a fourth player. Casey's idea for waiting and collecting water is a game Robert has played before and Robert immediately accepts it. Casey has offered a new pretend theme to initiate his entry into the play episode. The theme is accepted and elaborated upon on the basis of past experience, as a new player has negotiated his way into the game.

ENACTMENT PHASE OF THE EPISODE

"So it will go faster and faster and faster!" suggests Robert.

"That's a good idea," adds Ken, reinforcing the children's negotiation.

"The dam is break," Lawrence calls out, elaborating on the theme as water escapes from the dam.

"Oh no!" Casey says in a high-pitched and squeaky voice. "Look! The dam is breaking!"

Lawrence, Robert, and Casey crouch over the dam. They are quite close together as they all face inward.

"Look! It's gonna come out!" Casey yells. As Casey's voice gets higher in pitch, Raymond moves in next to Robert and peers into the water.

"I'm making two dams at once," Robert explains to Raymond as the play theme is further expanded.

Lawrence looks up across the water to the shelves where the large shovels are stored. He calls out, "Ahhh! I can—" He steps across the stream to get a shovel from the shelf. He returns to his spot by the side of the hill, slapping the sand. "This big shovel," he says in an engine motor voice, "can dig a dam. Ahhh! I use"—he pauses for emphasis—"this big shovel will block this dam."

"It's big!" adds Casey in a high, squeaky voice. Casey is getting dry sand from the hilltop.

"Ahhh! The water is coming fast. Dig the dam," says Lawrence.

Robert moves closer to the water. Ken leaves from where he has been observing and returns with a large real shovel. When he returns, Ken begins to dig as a player, explaining, "Well, before you have a dam, you need a place for the water to store up. It'd have to be *here*. Here could be the dam." As Ken demonstrates his plan, all other action stops as everyone watches the dam being quickly formed by Ken's efforts and his big shovel. By digging a large depression at the foot of the sand hill, Ken is creating a hole that will function as a lake behind the dam ("a place for the water to store up"). He then tells the children that together they can build the dam at the bottom end of the lake. Ken's strategy here is to localize the play by defining dam boundaries and building a large enough play space to accommodate all players.

Researchers have described the effect that such ecological support offers to children with the term *scaffolding*. Just as scaffolding on a building offers support to new structures, so, too, the ecology scaffolds for interactive play by providing thematic and linguistic cues that keep children playing together (see, for instance, Berk & Winsler, 1995; Bodrova & Leong, 1998; Ervin-Tripp, 1983; Pelligrini, 1982; Van Hoorn, Nourot, Scales, & Alward, 1999).

Ken explained during the tape screening that the integrity and duration of interactive events in the sand pit is directly related to the capacity of the area to hold players with the vividness of an actual "place." He is aware of children's attraction to water. During the screening of a later episode that same day, when the water had been turned off, group play appeared to decrease in the sand pit, and Ken observed, "Obviously the water was holding them." His comment reflects his perception of the fragility of episodes that do not have vivid cues to clearly articulate a play theme. Ken believes that to successfully maintain the duration of an episode, he needs to attract children with an interesting setup.

Ken's actions are interrupted by Lawrence: "But, but I have a big shovel too." Lawrence raises his shovel in emphasis. "I have a big shovel."

"Good for you. Then you can dig out big . . . big chunks of sand. Pretty heavy when they get wet," says Ken. He moves to a spot opposite the side from where he first was digging as he says to the players: "Then you need a dam across here too, right?" Ken is quickly shoveling up walls of sand into a lower dam.

Casey calls out to Ken, referring to him with someone else's name. "Ned, I digging me the color of Dilantin—I bet none of you is as brave as I am," he finishes quietly, referring to his recent cranial operation.

"Stop, Lawrence, you are messing up my . . . ," and Robert pauses to define his work. "My road," he continues. He smoothes and pats a length of sand in emphasis.

"We're making a daaaam!" Casey corrects, with some anxiety.

"It's gonna be a pretty big one," adds Ken.

"A pretty nice dam," says Casey as he digs the dammed water.

"Yeah," says Ken.

"Ken, I . . . I can break the dam," says Lawrence.

Raymond moves in and blocks Lawrence's actions with his shovel. "Don't!"

Casey wants to continue collecting water in anticipation of a dramatic release. "No! We want to make the water go really fast."

"Now, where—where's the water gonna go, when you break the dam? Which way you wait—" Ken adds quickly, not finishing his sentence in the excitement of the moment. Ken would like the children to plan their actions before impetuously breaking the dam.

"Over there, and over here," Robert answers.

"Both places?" Ken stops shoveling and steps back a few feet, watching.

"Yeah."

"O.K."

In preparation for further digging, Ken turns and walks around the perimeter of the sand pit, rather than through the play space. His actions again respect in a nonverbal way the actuality of the play theme as the current reality for the players. This is a dam, with a number of players working closely together building the dam walls. As an actual "place," it would be incongruous for Ken to step through such a construction area.

Ken moves away from the ecology.

Raymond looks up and notices Casey piling up sand to collect the water. "Hey, you blocked it."

"That's because I'm making another dam. I'm filling up this whole place," explains Casey. This comment serves to inform other players about his intention to create a second dam. Casey's commentary explains and integrates the play episode at this point. During screening interviews, Ken noted how successful Casey appeared in integrating the progression of developments within a play episode, due in large part to his use of commentary. He observed, "Casey seems to be providing the link on which the play is maintained." Casey is able to change and move the theme forward without disrupting the flow of the episode. In this sense, Ken felt that Casey provided a role similar to himself in verbally informing all players as to progressive developments: "Casey does what I do." Ken mentioned further that he relied on Casey to perform such an informative function during interactive play under his guidance.

Ken walks by the sand pit and asks in passing, "How's the dam goin'?"

"Let me help you. We're making a big hole, a big, a big, a big um . . . ," continues Raymond.

Casey responds to Ken's query. "Fine!" He then turns back to Raymond. "I know that. But this is heavy. It's a big heavy choke," he grunts, straining under the weight of a wet load of sand.

As Ken returns to the play space, he notices the large pool of water. "Oh boy, that's a big lake. Can a boat float on this lake?" As Ken moves in closer he notices Casey's dam. "Oh. You made a double dam. That's interesting." Ken's use of concrete labeling promotes future possible dialogue in relation to Casey's activities.

"You know what I'm doing? I'm filling up this whole place," says Casey. Ken's comment has prompted an immediate explanation of motives from Casey.

Meanwhile, Lawrence has dug out the dam, releasing the water. Lawrence is acting as a social scientist, as Gallas (1998) describes, "studying the effects of [his] behavior on others" (p. 44). He will studiously observe the consequences of his experimental actions. Throughout this study, Lawrence seeks to make sense of his world at school by intervening into ongoing play and watching for the results. Lawrence performed such experiments wherever he was. At the inside computer, he once called me over for assistance. The arrow keys were inexplicably making exactly opposite selections. I began to tear at my hair, feeling powerless against a viral infection in the software until I noticed the arrow keys had been popped off the keyboard and replaced backward. Lawrence was gleeful over my discovery.

Lawrence gets his expected rise in the sand pit.

"Oh no! No! Block the dam! Block the dam! We're not ready for it to go yet!" Ken bends forward and yells imperatively. Ken's adoption of a play voice and his use of "we" accompanies his conventional "call of alarm." The various verbal and nonverbal features of the interaction, supported by setup cues, richly frame the meaning to this interactive episode. Multiple cues help to assure that all players have probably noticed at least one of the many cues announcing progressions in the play theme.

Raymond moves next to Robert and Lawrence.

Lawrence quickly opens up the dam, making a grinding noise as he digs. "Urrrrr! Urrrr!"

Casey digs quickly on his own dam. "Oh no! My dam!" Casey says with alarm.

Ken interrupts Lawrence, piling sand on his break. "No, Lawrence! Lawrence! Don't! Don't do the dam until they—until everybody's ready! You gotta ask before you do it. When everybody's ready, then you can break the dam."

Lawrence notices a hole Ken has made in the sand by adding to the dam wall. "But you dig a deep hole."

Ken acknowledges the observation, but ignores it as a suggestion. "Yeah, I made a deep hole." Ken stands back from the dam. "You can work and build the dam higher," he says to Lawrence.

Lawrence begins again to break the dam. Ken interrupts this action, moving in again and placing his shovel in Lawrence's way. Ken is quite close to Lawrence's face as he addresses him. "Lawrence? Lawrence? Lawrence. Ask. Ask. Ask if they're ready for the dam to break." As Ken addresses Lawrence, all action around the dam ceases. Ken is structuring the terms of a negotiation between different play intentions among the players. He is intervening at the level of enactment, where the progression of the episode depends on management of this discrepancy of interests (specifically between Ken and Lawrence). When Lawrence continues to break open the dam wall, Ken heightens the forcefulness of his intervention by both physically blocking Lawrence's actions and moving in quite close in order to be directly face-to-face with Lawrence. Ken believes that the integrity and duration of this episode rests in maintaining the damming efforts. As an explicit teacher goal in this program, Ken is therefore quite intent on promoting such damming. All other activity in the play space ceases in reaction to the forcefulness of Ken's interruption.

"We can, ohhh, let the dam the break?" Lawrence asks.

With the full attention of all players, Ken now breaks down the structure of the negotiation further, providing Lawrence with specific language for making his intentions explicit to the group, "Say, say, 'Can we break the dam?'" offers Ken.

"Can we break the dam?"

"What do you guys say?" asks Ken.

"No!" says Casey quickly.

"What do you say, Robert?"

"No."

"No," repeats Ken.

Lawrence laughs and points as the dam breaks anyway under the pressure of the water. "The dam is break!"

"Oh no!" yells Casey.

"The little—" Ken pauses and considers how he wants to label the scene. "The upper dam broke," he adds. "Do you think the bottom dam's gonna break now?"

"No," says Robert.

"Quick! Quick!" Casey calls out. The water is, in fact, running out of the dam.

Robert notices and changes his mind: "Yes."

Ken begins digging with Casey. "Quick! Quick! Block it up. He needs help here!" Ken calls out in alarm. Dora is attracted to the ecology by all the excitement.

Raymond begins digging again at the dam.

"Quick, it's gonna explode. Really! Block, block it!" Casey yells in a very high and raspy voice.

Ken begins to dig, saying, "O.K. I'm gonna get this road—this all ready for when the dam breaks. I'm gonna get it all dug out. 'Cause I want the water to run down here." Ken's comment here marks a new development in the progression of the episode. He is demonstrating how a player informs other players as to his own actions and intentions. Because he is the teacher, however, it is unclear just how this demonstration is perceived by the children, who are of lower status.

What follows is three conversations occurring simultaneously as Lawrence, Casey, and Dora all talk separately to Ken until Dora suddenly notices a burst in the dam. "Raaaaaaaymoooooond! The dam's breaaaaaaakiiiiing!" she hollers.

Ken suggests, "Casey, you better keep—you better build that dam a little higher, 'cause it's gonna go over in a minute. See?"

"O.K., you help me, Ken," Casey suggests.

"Well, I can't." With the passing of the flood, the momentum of the game similarly diminishes. Casey, a strong leader in the games, looks to Ken for direction. Ken's role in the episode here is tricky. In the self-directed world of the play yard, the boundaries of teacher involvement vary with the style of the teacher. Ken is now aware that he may have involved himself too directly in the play and refrains from more direct participation. As the water builds up again, Ken attempts to step into an observer role, labeling the space and marking progressive developments with timed exclamations. From the children's perspective, however, the immediacy of Ken's pointed observations keep him intimately involved.

At the same time, Lawrence also notices the rupture. "Rrrrr! It's break!"

"Oh no!" Ken yells as the water flows out from the dam. "It's gotta be higher, I think."

"The dam is break!" Lawrence shouts.

The suspense is quite high now, prompting Ken to laugh. "You think it's breaking?"

"Oh! No!" cries Casey. "It's going right on my clothes! Quick! Quick, everybody! Better, you don't want to get wet?"

"Ahhh!" Lawrence whoops.

"Oh no!" says Ken, laughing.

"Oh no! Look at it go," Casey says as the water runs freely now out of the dammed area.

"Ahhh!" yells Lawrence again.

"It's too late!" warns Ken. "Watch out below. It's a flash flood! Watch out in the valley!"

"Now look it, look it. Look how fast it's going," Casey says to Ken in amazement.

"It's going super fast," agrees Ken.

"Break up the sand!" Casey comments as he observes the water speeding ahead.

Lawrence notices and laughs.

"The second dam is breaking," Ken announces. "Oh no! Look out below!"

"Ahhh!" shouts Lawrence. "It's, it's messing!"

"Look out below!" repeats Casey.

"I've never seen the water go so fast . . . you guys made some good dams," Ken adds.

"We need to make another dam. Look at this," says Casey.

"Kenny, I think we need your help," Dora says.

Ken stands up and moves into the dam area, as Casey, Raymond, and Dora begin to dig again. "Well, I'll need—I'll need to come back in and dig some of that wet sand out, that heavy wet sand for you guys, because . . ." Ken steps back into the player role, knowing that damming up will hold the interactive play episode together for a longer period of time. He again comments both on his actions and intentions in making a dam. "This'll be where the lake is. Right here. And we can make the dams around the lake. 'Cause when you make a dam, you have to make a place for the water to store up. Like a lake, or a reservoir."

Robert agrees with Ken, pointing where the lake should be. "Right here!"

"O.K."

As the children resume digging again, the children sing. The action is made mutual.

"I—I don't want to make a dam."

"I do."

"I love to make a dam."

"I do."

"I do!"

"I do!"

"I do!"

"I . . . I did it."

"I did."

"I do!"

"I do!"

"I do, I did, I did, I did it. I did."

"I do!"

Ken pulls back. Casey stands, looking repeatedly from the mud, in which he has been digging, to Ken. The action has quieted down considerably since the dam been rebuilt. "You're the um . . . you're the um . . . if you're just watching, who can you be?" asks Casey. As a researcher and a teacher, I had been analyzing this episode as one in which I felt Ken was strongly directing. It is interesting that Casey, as an actual player in this episode, perceives Ken as "just watching." Casey may indeed need Ken to be more involved on this particular day, the first day of his return from surgery. In fact, Casey has plans for Ken.

Ken responds, "If I'm just watching, who can I be? Um . . . ?"

"The architect," Casey suggests without hesitation.

"The architect, that's a good idea. I could be the architect, and you guys could be the engineers." During screening, Ken admitted to being quite uncomfortable with this assignment of roles, feeling unsure of how successful the children would be at independently managing such unfamiliar assignments.

"No, I don't want to be the engineer," Dora says.

"I, I . . . the engineer, too," says Lawrence.

"O.K."

Lawrence has misunderstood what kind of engineer Ken is referring to. Lawrence is thinking of a train engineer, and he now elaborates on an additional role for Ken in the train theme. "Eh, you be passenger on the engine, I be the really engineer."

"O.K. So . . ." Ken is so preoccupied with extracting himself as a directing player in the episode that he does not correct Lawrence here. "A good engineer tells his men what to do."

"I'm, I'm, I'm the, I'm the," Casey struggles, pausing to decide. "There are two engineers," Casey adds.

"Oh, O.K.," says Ken. "Well, I'm gonna be the man from the city." As Ken now assigns himself a role, he begins to walk away with determination. He returns, however, to explain what his role means. Ken is now facing into the dam area again. "I'm gonna be the man from the city, who oversees and makes sure that this city project gets done correctly."

"I want to be the really the one who tells them," says Dora.

"Well, you can be the architect, then. You can tell them how it's supposed to look," says Ken as he touches the top of Dora's head. He is trying to explain to the children the meaning of these role assignments.

He quickly turns and moves away. Ken said during the screening that he was quite uncomfortable, knowing they probably would not grasp their roles.

Lawrence turns and calls out to him. "I be the architect."

Ken calls out his response as he continues to move away from the area. Again he informs the players about role activities. "O.K. The architect tells them how it looks," he yells.

"I want to be the architect!" Dora yells back. The episode is deteriorating here with the assumption of unfamiliar roles.

Ken stops from across the opposite side of the sand pit, structuring the interaction again. "O.K., well there could be two. You have to work together with Lawrence though." He then pulls out of the pretend context to address Casey's wet clothes. "Casey, if you want to put a pair of shorts on, we can get you a pair of shorts."

"No."

Ken has moved off into another area of the yard. Dora calls out to him with urgency: "Is it too hot today?"

"It's very hot today," yells Ken.

The episode continues for another 32 minutes, with Ken reentering the play ecology every 2 to 5 minutes to repack the dam walls. While he is in the area, he offers commentary on his actions and intentions, and on observations of the intentions and actions of the players. Neither he nor the children refer to their role assignments, making that piece of the episode look more like a way that the children accommodated the retreat of Ken-as-player than a way that the children used to maintain the ongoing flow of the game.

During screening of this episode, Ken recalled feeling frustrated that the episode did not "take off better." He recalled that the year before, a different set of children had been able to play in a much more elaborate and independent fashion. Based on his experience from the prior year, Ken said he "expected more self-direction" from the children. Looking at himself on the videotape, Ken felt that he had to direct much of the episode in order for it to progress.

REVIEW OF THE EPISODE

This episode is thematically typical of a wet sand ecology where children negotiate individual plans based on a common theme. In this episode, the children both jostle for control and share control with other playmates as they regulate the flow and breakage of water. A singsong routine emerges twice in the episode to mark points of mutuality. The singsong routine "Goody mud butt" initiates the episode in focused attention as the stream theme is suggested and immediately repeated in acknowledged acceptance. The singsong "I want to build a dam" serves to further the play episode as the theme is developed and modified. The singsong routine works to integrate players around a mutually agreed-upon and familiar theme.

Channeling and stopping rivers are frequent themes in the sand pit ecology. Ken sets up the area knowing and capitalizing on this shared experience. Robert quickly agrees to Casey's inclusion as a player in making a dam partly because Ken has set up the area to capitalize on the children's need for repetition of pretend themes. In repetition, the children have the opportunity to master skills, experience success, and feel accomplished.

In addition to thematic cues from Ken's setup, signals for "this is pretend" involve changes in tone of voice, use of sound effects, descriptive commentary, and the attempted adoption of roles. Changes of voice register for the most part involve a high-pitched voice tone marking the pretend nature of the interaction, as well as the fantasy theme of alarm. Ken, as a participant in the episode, himself uses changes in the tone of his voice to signal new information and theme changes in the episode's progression. For example, he raises his voice to suggest a delay in water release: "Oh, no! No! Block the dam! We're not ready for it to go yet!" The children are also using shifts in voice tone throughout the episode. The children use sound effects to accompany and highlight important pretend action, as when Lawrence arrives with a shovel and uses a motor voice to announce "The big shovel can dig a dam." Explanatory comments, like Lawrence's, are used by both Ken and the children to describe thematic action and progress, as was the case in "Making a New Road." Toward the end of the transcribed portion of the episode, the children signal "this is pretend" with the explicit adoption of pretend roles, marked by the preliminary phrases "You be—" and "I'm the—". For example, "You be passenger on the engine, I be the really engineer" and "I'm, I'm, I'm the, I'm the . . . there are two engineers."

The episode includes a number of sophisticated features. Lawrence adopts the role of a big shovel. Numerous announcements are made like "The dam is breaking" to mark the pretend theme as water runs into the sand. Casey elaborates with a description to mark the pretend action by saying, "I'm making another dam. I'm filling up this whole place." Ken structures a negotiation regarding discrepant needs to break or build up the dam. There is hypothesizing about the effects of the release of water. There is the recognition by the children that role adoption is useful as the episode progresses, though the roles of architect and landscape engineer do not readily lend themselves to familiar and easily identified role-related behavior. The episode includes instances where the children communicate in turn on the progress of the pretend theme, allowing for elaboration of the activity. When Casey got wet, the children shift between fantasy and reality, with the episode continuing despite the reality of Casey's clothes. In these instances, the sophistication of pretend provides the children with the opportunity to think flexibly, entertain multiple perspectives, suggest alternatives, and elaborate on the play theme.

Ken adopts a number of strategies, initially *organizing the environment* and then following up throughout the episode by returning to the ecology regularly to *restore* the walls of the dam and thereby extend the duration of this particularly long episode. Ken's direct participation shifts between two strategies: play tutor and spectator. As a player in the game, Ken is more in line with the *play tutor* strategy of Smilansky (1968). In his role as player, Ken suggests ideas, uses language that encourages clarification and negotiation of the theme, and models play action. The role of play tutor is the strongest, most directive strategy a teacher can adopt. Ken adopts a directorial role with the intent of prolonging the duration of the episode, which he successfully does. Ken himself is uncomfortable with the influential level of his involvement, recognizing that the children are not operating with self-direction in the episode. In following the episode, it appears that Ken only becomes a play tutor when the play episode threatens to dissipate. If a teacher's primary goal is to maintain the duration of the play episode, becoming a play tutor can be effective. The strategy of play tutor is intended specifically to train children in adopting pretend play by modeling language, using props and roles, and suggesting ideas to elaborate, all of which Ken does. On two occasions Ken's forceful direction has the effect of halting all action. Ken does try to extricate himself to promote autonomous play by becoming the man from the city. He casts himself in a supporting role where he functions as a *spectator* who comments on the theme-as-real to extend the episode's length. The shift to "man from the city" as spectator makes sense, though Ken does not assume the role of architect. Casey assigns it to him. Then Ken suggests other roles that the children debate, negotiate, and adopt. In the final anecdotal chapter, Chapter 5, it is demonstrated how Karen supports play as a spectator as well, commenting on play action while remaining outside any player role.

5 Two Guys

Credit: **Bob Devaney**

THIS EPISODE IS a reflection of the vigilance and unpredictability inherent in young children's interactions. Vigilance and unpredictability together create a quality of fragility in the peer play, determining much of the behavior and themes included in this episode. Carl will continuously vie for the undivided attention of his friend Warren. A resulting chase game emerges to assure participation and some measure of control among the players. Just as Seth, Danny, and Chris continually negotiated the subtleties of partner inclusion, so, too, is Carl concerned throughout this play episode with Warren's attention. Carl continually refers to his alliance with Warren, using stereotyped and intimate shorthand to remind Warren of the shared context of their game.

As a pair, these boys are almost always involved in pretend play. They play most often outside. They are able to change the location of their play activity without any disruption to their fantasy. They have no trouble maintaining a consistent fantasy theme even though the physical cues around them are often changing as they roam. Children who can change the location of their play and still retain their specific fantasy theme more often than not are using language, rather than location, to keep their play theme going. Usually roles are identified: "We're playing Power Rangers and I'm the black one." Warren and Carl, however, use sounds, single words, and stereotyped phrases, rather than specifically identified roles. The language between these two players is not very advanced. Nonetheless, these players are doing something to hold their game together not only across changing physical cues, but also for long stretches of time.

Warren, age 4 years, 7 months, and Carl, age 4 years, 10 months, play a familiar game of dramatic rescue, in part influenced by the dominant height of the large climber and its wide slide. A hanging bar, across the top of the slide, figures prominently in this episode. In this game, Warren and Carl yell in mock distress, as if hanging from a cliff. One or both will lie hanging from the top of the slide, or lie on the slide. Corsaro (1985) identifies this dramatic scenario as one of three themes that regularly appear in the peer play of young children: lost-found, danger-rescue, and death-rebirth. Warren and Carl are using autonomous play to address the danger and rescue theme. Besides Warren and Carl, other players in this episode include Lawrence, age 4 years, 6 months; Dora, age 5 years, 2 months; and Marta, age 4 years, 10 months. The supervising teacher on this day is Karen. This play episode lasts 12 minutes.

INITIATION AND NEGOTIATION PHASES OF THE EPISODE

Warren climbs up the slide and calls out, *"Carl!"* He breaks his graham crackers into small pieces and drops them into a paper cup. He calls out loudly again, adding an adornment. *"Carlie!"*

Carl shouts as he crosses the yard past Karen, sweeping. He moves to the large climber area. "Guy! *Guy!*" Carl's response confirms that he agrees to play with Warren. Carl is also suggesting a theme to their play by referring to Warren as "Guy."

Warren responds, "Hi, Guy," thus accepting Carl's role suggestion. The initiation and negotiation phases of the episode occur virtually simultaneously here as these children nearly always play together in some danger fantasy. Corsaro (1985) notes the saliency of the danger theme for controlling that which is fearsome. While adopting the role "Guy," Warren and Carl have recognized their shared history of playing danger games, but have yet to negotiate how they will play the theme today.

"Whatcha doing—" Carl begins, then notices that Warren has graham crackers. "Yeah, that's what I just want . . ."

"No, it's *mine!*"

Carl walks up the slide toward Warren, shifting his request into the world of pretend: ". . . Guy, that's . . . I . . . I already . . . but . . . I need powerballs."

Warren rejects Carl's request. "Ooo, *too late.*" Even though Carl adopts fantasy to gain compliance, Warren remains unmoved.

Carl initiates the negotiated theme, faking a fall as he grasps for the top of the slide. "Ahh!"

Warren forcefully rejects Carl's attempt to enact the play theme. "*Go!*"

Carl climbs up to the platform and sits directly across from Warren. He pauses momentarily as he looks at Warren and waits. Getting no acknowledgment whatsoever, Carl announces his leave-taking. "I'm not gonna play with you anymore. . . . Bye, bye!"

Warren does not respond to Carl's announcement, and Carl goes down the slide. Most children do not mark their leave-taking as a courteous social convention that adults observe. Leave-taking serves a different function for young children. In this case, Carl is using his announcement to stay connected to Warren.

Now on the ground, Carl speaks softly, almost to himself: "I'm moving to a *neeeew* house." He moves to an adjacent climbing structure.

Still eating his cracker, Warren watches, then stands up and yells loudly: "I'm gonna give ya' a tout, bitch. Birdbrain head!"

Carl responds with equal force from the confines of his own separate dwelling: "Stay there!" Carl adds this next thought too quietly for Warren to hear: "I'm . . . you're not killing me."

Warren yells out again to Carl. "*That's* it! I'm gonna fight wich ya!"

Carl runs to the bottom of the slide, accepting Warren's challenge. "Oh, yeah?" Planting himself firmly at the bottom of the slide, Carl winds up for a swing at Warren, who is sliding down to meet him. They struggle, embellishing their wrestle with grunting sound effects that are synchronized with their movements. "Huh!" "Arrr!" "Uh!"

Carl lets go, looking at Karen. Warren pushes Carl to the ground. During screening, Karen explains that she did not see the fistfight until after it had been going on for a while.

With hands on his hips, Warren accosts Carl: "You little bitch."

Carl, from the ground, brushes off his leg and foot. He gets up and the two boys swing and hit each other four more times, grunting.

Carl throws Warren to the ground.

Karen walks over to the large climber. "*Carl* . . . ? Are you guys really fighting, or are you just pretending?" She is asking for information, not having seen the circumstances that led to this altercation. It is a school rule that children cannot hurt each other. During screening, Karen explains that she often will simply ask for a child's perspective on a situation when she either has not seen or is not sure of what is happening.

Warren brushes himself off as Carl approaches Karen.

Lawrence, who is observing nearby, offers an explanation for Carl's actions. "He . . . he's the *robber!*"

With mild surprise, Karen asks Carl, "Oh, what *happened?*"

Warren crawls up the slide. Warren and Carl's ease here is noticeable given the fact that they have clearly broken a school rule against fighting.

Karen sits next to Carl on the bottom of the slide, listening attentively as Carl speaks. "He . . . I was not try and get his graham crackers but he said I was gonna—"

Karen interrupts in order to clarify Carl's interpretation. "He thought—"

Carl tries to finish but has trouble explaining. "I was gonna . . ."

Karen mildly and slowly seeks verification of her understanding: "He thought you . . . were trying to get his graham crackers?"

Carl corrects her firmly. *"No."*

Karen acknowledges his correction. "Oh."

"I was not trying to, but Warren . . . I have . . . I was into a big fight with him." Carl ends his final statement in a tone of honest surprise, punctuating "big fight" with a swing of his fist.

Karen responds with equally abashed and incredulous surprise. "I *saw* that." She pauses to look up at Warren. "You guys were punching each other. So, Warren? Are you still angry at Carl?"

During the screening, Karen explains, "Somehow from the conversation I got that Carl wanted something and Warren wouldn't give it to him, so that it was really *Warren* who was the victim, more or less."

Warren readily responds as he hangs from the crossbar. "No."

Lawrence enters under the slide. Carl gets up and climbs up the slide toward Warren. Warren slides down to meet Carl, grabbing hold of him. Both struggle to regain an upward climb.

Karen attempts a final conclusion: "Do you think, maybe if you guys get angry with each other, you should talk to each other . . . instead of hitting each other?"

Carl yells out to Warren. "Ahh!"

Warren hangs on Carl. "Errh." With the altercation behind them, Warren and Carl have immediately returned to the danger theme. Karen moves away slightly and watches.

Warren yells a request to Carl. "Arh! Gimme!"

Carl grabs for Warren's hand, switching back to the role referent. "Guy, what? Got you!"

Warren slips downward, then both boys scramble to the top of the slide. They hang, turning to look face-to-face as they call out in distress. Having explicitly agreed on a danger theme, albeit with vague verbal description and unspecified "Guy" role, the episode moves into the enactment phase.

ENACTMENT PHASE OF THE EPISODE

The bond between Carl and Warren now reassured, they scramble to the top of the climber. Warren reminds Carl about the crackers: "Arh! Yay. Don't take any of my power."

Carl responds with an elaboration: "Where's all my power? Somebody has my power!" His tone is slightly higher than normal. Carl's adoption of a higher register serves the function of signaling lower status to prompt Warren's allegiance to him. Like Raymond and Matthew in the "Needles" episode, Carl is suggesting an external challenge in his play interaction with Warren. As Lawrence reaches the upper deck, Warren begins to wrestle with him.

"Don't catch me," directs Lawrence.

Carl breaks from the fantasy in order to dissuade Lawrence from staying. "Go down, Lawrence, I don't want you."

Lawrence correctly senses a difference in play intentions between Carl and Warren. Warren has already included Lawrence in the game with a familiar wrestling repertoire. Carl is not as accommodating.

Lawrence struggles as he and Warren continue to wrestle. "But Warren . . . Warren is catch . . . Warren catch me . . . Warren is catch . . ." For Warren, Lawrence's timing offers the perfect casting to the part of robber.

Carl, having suggested an external challenge, is nonetheless not willing to accept a new player into the game. He tries to block this development with the initiation of a number of stereotyped postures and vocalizations to draw Warren's attention back. He moves on all fours. He yells, swinging from the bar: "Guy! Aah!" He yells a second and then a third time.

Warren finally returns the yell, catching Carl's glance: "Ahh!" Warren has confirmed his recognition of the familiar theme. He releases Lawrence. Seeing Dora and Marta arrive, he goes down the slide yelling: "Come on! Dora!"

He is interrupted by Carl's yell: "Ahh!"

Warren stops on the bottom of the slide: "Dora! Get *him*!"

Warren wants Dora to "get" Lawrence. Warren is negotiating an elaboration of the danger theme to include capture.

Lawrence slides down the slide, knocking Warren over on top of him. Dora, Marta, and Lawrence laugh. Karen, observing from a distance, notices this action but does not come over. During the screening, I asked her why she didn't approach this apparently unsafe activity. She said that at the time of its occurrence the incident naturally resolved itself and the play episode had moved on into other action. Karen's intention here is to maintain safety while supporting the continuity of the play interaction, especially for Lawrence, who is beginning to sustain independent interactive exchanges with other children.

Pelligrini and Smith (1998) speak to a feature of any play yard that contributes to the complexity Karen is honoring. In its spaciousness, outdoor ecologies support running, chasing, fleeing, and wrestling. Pelligrini (1995) notes that such activity, called rough-and-tumble, can be distinguished from aggression in its behavior, consequences, structure, and the ecologies where it is likely to occur. Teachers in the play yard become keen observers of the differences between rough-and-tumble and aggression, the latter which includes closed-hand hits, shoves, pushes, and kicks. Following a bout of rough-and-tumble play, children continue in the interaction, often cooperatively. Aggression, however, usually results in the players separating. The alternation of roles in pretend play readily complements rough-and-tumble play (Pelligrini, 1993), where players switch between chaser and chasee; whereas in aggression, players do not switch roles. Rough-and-tumble play is more likely to occur outside where areas are spacious, while aggression is likely to occur inside or out. By encouraging Lawrence's participation in rough-and-tumble play, Karen is supporting practice in language, cooperation, and perspective-taking.

Dora laughs with Marta about Lawrence's collision with Warren: "Yeah. That's so funny."

Warren remains at the bottom, expressing his displeasure to Lawrence: "Take blow up, Dude!"

Lawrence runs away, laughing. Dora and Marta follow him over to Karen.

Carl suggests regrouping: "Let's get it back up here." Both Carl and Warren return up the slide.

Lawrence seeks out Karen. Teachers in this classroom often impose a "down only" rule on the slide to ensure safety when a large group is on the climber. Lawrence notes to Karen, "Warren up the slide." He wants help entering the play interaction at the slide. He does this by calling Karen's attention to a behavior he thinks requires intervention.

Karen accepts Lawrence's observation, but focuses on Lawrence, rather than on Warren. "Yeah, I don't want you to push Warren on the slide."

Dora remarks on the humor of the event to Karen. "He was standing up. It's funny!"

Karen does not dispute the humor of the event. She nonetheless stresses the issue of safety. "Well, it wouldn't have been funny if he had fallen off."

Dora then elaborates on the context of the interaction between Lawrence and Warren: "Lawrence was fighting with Warren."

Karen does not respond to Dora's last comment here. Her strategy, instead, is to focus on the issue of safety while at the same time remaining neutral regarding other occurrences in the episode. Karen's neutrality serves the purpose of ensuring safety while encouraging Lawrence's involvement in pretend play with others.

Back at the large climber, Carl suggests, "Let's go, Guy! Yee-ah!"

Having reinvoked the play theme with the referent "Guy," Carl waits for Warren at the top of the slide. Warren does not respond, and Carl swings out over the slide from the crossbar a number of times, hitting his feet on the slide on the backswing. Carl then stops swinging, and sits at the top of the slide to watch Lawrence return with Dora and Marta following, laughing.

Marta wants Lawrence to make them laugh again. "I hope he does it again."

Lawrence turns around to look at Dora and Marta, then climbs up the large climber.

Warren, seeing Lawrence's advancement, climbs up the slide.

"Lawrence, can you do that again?" asks Dora.

"Karen said *nooo*," reminds Lawrence.

Dora persists, "So, Lawrence, what do you want to do another funny joke to? Show Marta? Can't you?"

Dora and Marta have yet to interact in this episode from within the context of any play theme.

Warren slides down with Lawrence growling in pursuit. "Rrrr!" They run off to the inside classroom with Carl following.

Dora and Marta laugh in mutual amusement.

Karen calls out to Lawrence as he passes by. She does not address either Warren or Carl. "Lawreeence!" Karen is concerned here with the activity of chasing. Her intention is to allow only a certain level of movement in the yard for safety reasons. For her standards, chasing is not acceptable as an activity. During the screening, Karen was impressed with her own skills at observation here, correctly identifying Lawrence as the player who had been chasing the others. It is for this reason that Karen seeks out only Lawrence for questioning.

Dora and Marta climb up the ladder. "Gonna do another funny," Marta says.

"Ahr! I wonder what he'll do?" adds Dora.

Seeing Carl, Warren, and Lawrence returning from the inside class-room, Marta moves quickly to the top of the slide and slides down. "Let's go, let's go."

Dora yells out but remains on top of the climber. The return of the boys has triggered a runaway routine for Marta. When Marta sees the three boys getting closer, she climbs back up the climber next to Dora and reinforces their mutual theme by shouting, "Let's go!"

Karen enters the slide area following Warren and Carl. As Warren and Carl scamper up the slide, Karen calls out to get their attention. "You know what, Warren and Carl? I told Lawrence that if he wanted to play with you guys, he should play with you and not chase you. O.K.? 'Cause somebody will end up in trouble for running and then they'll have to go inside, so . . ." Karen's remarks establish a rule for interacting in this episode, which includes both localizing the activity and doing something she calls "play-ing with." Without any further elaboration, she sets up an expectation for interactive play in her area that involves interacting together but not run-ning. She leaves the decision as to the quality and context of such interac-tive activity to Dora, Marta, Warren, Carl, and Lawrence and again moves away. Karen fully expects that the children will understand her directive.

"I didn't run," Dora says.

Carl almost bumps into Warren at the bottom of the slide. "Move!" He looks at Warren. "Watch where you're going!" he says with real irrita-tion. Carl may be feeling put out here at Karen's suggestion that Lawrence play with both him and Warren.

Lawrence now slides down the slide. "Rrrr. I slide down."

Warren moves out of his way mid-slide, but grabs for Lawrence as Lawrence passes, immediately initiating the danger theme again.

"Warren, try to catch me," Dora suggests, interjecting herself into the game.

Warren slides down to Dora. "I got a vest on." He does not directly address Dora's request to catch her, instead choosing to show off a prized piece of clothing.

Again Carl intercedes between the conversation of Warren and another to evoke the original danger theme. "Arhhh!" Carl is lying down, dangling from the top lip of the slide, looking to Warren and yelling out cries of dramatic distress. Warren returns the glance. Their dyadic interaction is tightly focused on familiar fantasy.

Dora moves to Lawrence. "Ooo, Lawrence! Boo!" She kisses him loudly. Warren yells in reaction to Dora's kiss. The play group begins a series of descents and ascents with the danger theme having a provoca-tive, new element—the kiss.

Corsaro (1985) identifies cross-gender approach-avoidance play in young children. This game is much like Raymond's and Matthew's "feigned fear" in "Needles." It occurs in part because the ecology is conducive to dramatically quick exits, due to the height and double width of the slide. The interaction surfaces Dora's developing awareness of how girls and boys act toward each other. Unlike "Needles," where Lawrence was not a willing party to the chase, Dora is ready to join. Carl, however, slows the pace.

"I fell down," he cries.

Warren responds with affinity: "Oh, brother."

Dora stands on the bottom of the slide. She watches Warren and Carl. The quick ascending and descending has ceased. She laughs abruptly, then climbs halfway up the slide and slides down in mock alarm. "Ahhh!" Warren and Carl do not respond. Dora tries a different approach. She lies facedown in a "fallen" pose on the bottom of the slide. A "fallen" pose, dramatically motionless, suggests serious injury and often death in the pretend world of the peer culture. It almost always evokes caretaking and/or attention. Dora lifts her head to look up to the platform, then flips over on her back to again lie "fallen."

Lawrence, oblivious to the consequences, slides down. "Eeeeou!"

Sensing the impending collision below, Warren calls out: "Crash your butt!" Warren's comment here adds a further provocative element to that one initiated by Dora's kiss, the "butt."

Lawrence slides into Dora.

Dora nervously laughs: "Wow."

Warren also slides down and runs into Lawrence as Marta yells, "Crash your—eeee!" Lawrence exits the ecology. At this point in the episode, the charge on the topics of kissing and crashing butts has overtaken any progression or development of the original theme. The provocative nature of these topics is one the children are not prepared to develop. They know kissing as a routine that most usually occurs with a parent, another family member, or in the context of a family friendship situation. Bottoms usually get attended to during toileting. In both cases, the pretend element involves assuming a role of higher or lower stature congruent with the children's experience. The game will not develop because the children are all involved as equal status peers. Were Dora to become "the mommy" or someone else to assume a "baby," the game could continue by incorporating these elements. It is because the children are playing in equal-status roles that the provocative nature of the kiss and the butt is so charged.

The children, in fact, are playing with the excitement that such topics evoke. The possibly dangerous pileup at the bottom of the slide and Marta's loud squeal both point to such excitement. The children are in the midst of trying to make sense of what they have, no doubt, picked up from the world of stories, visual media, and adult interaction. They don't know why kissing and bottoms are charged, but they have experienced the charge.

"Crash your butt," Warren punctuates.

Dora has hurt her finger in the crash. She rubs her hand. "Ow!"

Marta watches from the top of the slide as Carl, with irritation, tries to get around her in order to slide down.

"Let *go!*" he cries.

Dora is still rubbing her hand in discomfort. "Ow!"

Carl repeats his request just as forcefully: "Lemme go!"

Dora continues at the base of the slide: "Ow. Ow."

Marta slides down to Dora. "You O.K.?"

"It hurts."

Carl slides down the slide, punctuating his descent with a couple of dramatic yells. "Wow . . . ahhh!" Carl reintroduces the original danger theme. He pauses briefly to look at Dora and Marta before returning up the climber.

Marta now gives Dora some specific advice. "Press on it. Press on it very lightly and kind of slightly, O.K., Dora?"

Dora, now recovered, climbs halfway up the slide.

Warren slides down next to her, catching onto her legs as she lays midslide, firmly grabbing hold of the slide's edge. Grabbing legs is characteristic of his play with Carl.

Dora calls out in real distress, "Help!" She is losing her grip and does not like being pulled by Warren.

Warren hears her call and interprets it within the danger theme. He immediately goes to her rescue. "I got ya!" For Warren, the theme is triggered by Dora's stereotyped action of dangling down the surface of the slide. Warren's response "I got ya" is intended to convey safety, though in fact, Warren does not have hold of her, but is hanging *from* Dora's ankles as they dangle together down the surface of the slide.

Warren's actions are too much for Dora, and she rejects the play, raising her voice in distress and irritation: "Don't, Waaarr*eeen*!" The force of her rising shrill tone and her use of Warren's name conveys her real feelings outside of the play theme.

Warren releases his hold, and they both slide slowly down the slide. Dora's tone is an example of how children use shifts in register to contextualize their interactions during play. Just as in the dam-building episode, the play voice is a cue to the episode's progress. Here, a change in voice tone marks a shift back to the real world.

Marta is scared by Dora's shriek. "Should I get the teacher?"

Warren tries to drown out Marta's remark: "Ahhhhh!" He is displeased at being misunderstood and angry that he may be tattled on. Invoking the authority of the teacher is as much a one-upmanship between peers as it is a plea for assistance.

"Yes," Dora replies to Marta in a small yelp.

Marta does not leave, however, but rather remains next to Dora. The one-upmanship has been accomplished without the aid of the teacher's authority.

Warren reaches the bottom of the slide. He turns to directly face Dora. "Stupid brat!" He then climbs back up the climber. He is clearly put out and deflated from the original excitement of the drama as he had understood it. He attempts to wrestle with Carl in a reinitiation of the original theme, but he is too rough.

"Stop, Warren!" yells Carl sternly.

Karen, who has been monitoring the action from a distance, now moves in at the point where safety becomes an issue: "Warren, that's not safe. Don't push kids on the slide or you'll have to get off." Again, Karen's strategy is to focus on the specific behaviors in question. She nonetheless adds a cautionary threat. Pushing on the slide is a strictly unacceptable behavior well understood by the children. Karen is reminding Warren of her inflexibility here.

Warren makes a rude sound immediately following Karen's remarks.

Marta climbs down next to Karen. "Warren called Dora a spoiled brat."

As Marta "tells on" Warren, Warren dangles on the surface of the slide and yells loudly over her words: "Ahhhhhh!" Warren would much prefer returning to the familiar and emotionally safer danger theme he is accustomed to playing with Carl.

Karen responds to Marta's tattling with the same tone of surprise and interest she used in listening to Carl explain his fight with Warren much earlier. "He di-id?" She then directs her questioning to speculating about Warren's action. "Do you know what he means?"

Marta shakes her head "no."

"I don't either," Karen says. Karen has responded to Marta's accusation by speculating on Warren's intentions, rather than directly reprimanding Warren. Like Ken, who did not respond directly to Lawrence's report of Raymond's misconduct in "Needles," Karen also shifts her response in order to wonder about Warren's perspective. "If he calls you names, just say, tell him it's not nice to call people names," she adds.

Dora reassures Karen of her innocence. "See, I . . . he called me names but I didn't call him names." The episode ends here when Carl and Warren, the two original participants, leave the slide area to continue the game at the tire swing. Marta and Dora ascend the slide, continuing to chat as they survey the yard. Lawrence has been noticeably absent since the crashing butts incident, having tranformed from a fighter to a lover before his departure. His participation is more active and integrated than, for example, his role in Raymond and Matthew's game in Chapter 2.

REVIEW OF THE EPISODE

This episode is a good example of outdoor rough-and-tumble play as described by Blurton-Jones (1976). Such play includes running, chasing, wrestling, laughing, and falling, among other behaviors. Marta attempts to elaborate the game into a more clearly defined chase game, but she does not get Dora's participation. When Dora kisses Lawrence, she transforms the relatively nonverbal roles of the original danger game into more complex roles of gender. Dora is superimposing on the interaction her developing appreciation of what it means to be a girl and how boys and girls act with one another.

Corsaro (1985) notes the importance of cross-gender approach-avoidance play in young children's development of social knowledge. Dora attempts involvement first by kissing and then by soliciting care as an injured party. Carl, however, is not prepared to include other players in the interaction. Warren is ready to include Dora, but only at the level of chasing, wrestling, falling, and vocalizing play. Dora's "fallen" pose would require the adoption of caretaking or medical roles, which Carl and Warren are not yet prepared to do. The episode ends in player dissatisfaction. There is also the element of competition between Carl and Dora for Warren's attention. One might wonder how much of the episode involves the rejection of cross-gender play because Warren is not ready and how much of the episode is a matter of Warren choosing between Carl, his frequent playmate, and Dora.

And Lawrence? In this game, Lawrence is the guy who gets kissed. Lawrence is the guy who slides down on the fallen angel. In an ironic turn of roles that evokes the poetry of such pretend play, Lawrence is the actor in both of the most complex instances of pretend play in the episode. He reacts by exiting the scene. Dora wants to play with Warren because he is obliging. And Marta delivers poetic attention and etiquette as the guardian to her fallen partner, lest Dora stray too far afield in her gendered adventures.

The episode provides numerous examples of how children signal and negotiate "this is pretend" from "this is real." The phrase "Guy!", when called out by Warren or Carl, is a signal not only that "this is pretend" but that a specific game with shared significance is being suggested or affirmed. Dora uses the fallen pose to elaborate the pretend theme, albeit unsuccessfully. The ritualized dangle from the slide, accompanied by "Ahhh!" is another signal for the shared game. Warren misinterprets Dora's intentions when she inadvertently sends the dangle signal.

As a cognitive skill, signals of "pretend" or "real" involve sophisticated shifts between the real world of objects and people and the fantasy world of transformations. The shift between reality and fantasy occurs throughout this episode. Karen prompts Carl and Warren for the distinction when they are fighting at the bottom of the slide. The ritualized stance of the two boys makes it difficult for Karen to interpret whether their actions are "play" or "real." Carl registers discomfort with the entry of a third player by addressing Lawrence from outside the play theme: "Go down, Lawrence, I don't want you." Players are referred to sternly by name when the rough-and-tumble play feels uncomfortable, as when Dora shifts from the "get me" game of dangling and grabbing to the real signal of referring to Warren by name. Her tone of voice reinforces and clarifies the fact that "this is real," and she wants Warren to stop the play.

Warren and Carl's use of idiosyncratic signals is a clue to their ability to successfully integrate their fantasy play across different play ecologies. They use an array of familiar signals to mark play. These signals are diffuse enough to be independent of the specific context of each day's scenario or setting. "Ahhh!" and "Guy!" can be easily transferred across many play areas, as happens at the end of the episode when the two move to the tire swing. More importantly, however, both playmates enjoy an especially loyal and interdependent history of playing mostly with just each other. As a result, they are less prone to suffer the unpredictability that usually characterizes play interactions at this age. "Ahhh!" and "Guy!" are private signals in the peer culture that not only symbolize the allegiance between Warren and Carl, but connote the peer culture theme of danger. While an implied theme, the danger is nevertheless undeniable. When the children build dams and drive trucks, these are obviously not real dams and full-size trucks. When they play at being architects, engineers, and the man from the city, they obviously are not really architects. They are pretending. In these instances, fantasy is defined as using physical props to represent real-life activities and assuming roles to represent real-life roles. But fantasy can also operate on less defined ground. What distinguishes the real world of hitting, chasing, and dangling from a fantasy version of the same activities? Karen wonders the same thing when she asks, "Are you guys really fighting or just pretending?"

Smilansky's (1968) six features of pretend play with peers, introduced in Chapter 1, bears repeating here:

1. Children match play behavior with adopted pretend roles.
2. Children use make-believe objects to substitute for real objects and use verbal utterances to represent action.

3. Children describe make-believe action in the course of coordinating the game.
4. Children persist in a play episode for at least 10 minutes.
5. The play involves at least two children engaged in pretend.
6. Children verbally interact in the course of play, usually to clarify or negotiate.

Warren and Carl adopt the pretend role of "Guy." It is an idiosyncratic role that designates allegiance, rather than a familial or vocational role that has readily identifiable behaviors matched to it. Behaviors matched to the "Guy" role involve paying attention to the pretend distress of your partner and perhaps giving your partner a hand. It also involves trying to save yourself from the forces of gravity. The slide may still be the slide, but it is imbued with the danger of gravity when one is dangling on its surface with a precarious grip. Warren and Carl's pretend game is not to slide down the slide on their bottoms and land firmly on their feet. The height of the slide communicates danger for anyone willing to adopt it in pretend play.

Warren and Carl use calls to present the action of being in distress. They do not, however, describe make-believe action in the course of coordinating the game. We never hear, for example, "This guy's trying to get up the mountain." Warren and Carl are content to play with the pretend theme of danger without articulating an actual place. Developmentally they have yet to reach the stage where they can describe their pretend environment like Danny, Casey, Seth, and even Lawrence can. For Warren and Carl, the ritualized, repetitive behavior of dangling and calling out is effective, because language is not yet available.

The episode persists for 12 minutes, with Warren and Carl retaining their danger theme. There is significant verbal interaction amongst the two "guys," and Carl, Dora, and Marta as the danger theme is understood or misunderstood and as a new theme of "boy" and "girl" is interjected.

Van Hoorn and her colleagues (1999) offer a continuum of teaching strategies that range from the very indirect, such as setup and maintenance of the ecology, to the very direct, such as the play tutor. Karen's supervision provides an example of the many roles one may adopt in the play yard. Karen maintains an *observer* role throughout this episode, distinctly refraining from interaction to encourage the children's autonomous skills in problem solving and mediation. When the play escalates physically in what looks like real hitting and pushing, Karen moves in as a *peacemaker*, soliciting information on motives and reflecting genuine acceptance of the children's interpretation. To promote focused interaction and reduce the risk of injury, Karen encourages Lawrence to stop running and to "play with" Warren and Carl. As an *artist apprentice* strategy, where clutter around an ongoing play event is removed, Karen recognizes and protects the play at the large climber by discouraging chasing that might mean an end to the game due to dispersal. The clutter in this case is fast-paced back-and-forth, running in and out of the ecology, which can serve as a distraction.

THE PRIMACY OF THE PLAY EPISODE

In my work as both a teacher and researcher, children's play interactions in the yard are the most salient classroom events. Rather than observing children and their developing skills and abilities exclusively, I am interested in the play episode as a distinct event that describes the perspectives of the children's peer culture. What does it mean for a group of children who run carefree around the sand pit, laughing and smiling broadly in paraded pursuit, then return to the shelter of a stand-in cube, only to repeat this activity numerous times that day and then repeat the game over a number of days? The progression of a play episode is not just a convention of my work as a researcher, but a salient frame for all teachers to use when observing in the yard. I see the play episode, and its progressive development using Scales's three points of initiation, negotiation, and enactment as an event that teachers can use to cultivate autonomy from the children's perspective.

Most often children's individual needs reveal themselves in the context of the peer group. I understand, for example, primitive attempts at "initiating" when I see unfocused running and shrieking. While this behavior can get on my nerves, I understand the behavior pattern in the context of a need for affiliation. How can I help this child experience satisfactory interactions with peers? Following the children through these anecdotal chapters, I am clear that children's linguistic skills can best be developed in manageable groups of between three and four playmates, where negotiating skills can reasonably be tried and practiced. I create protected and defined areas for play groups to locate so that social and intellectual skills can be enacted and realized. Sharing the play yard with children includes honoring the vivid life of the peer play episode. In Chapter 6, I outline the subtle decision-making process involved in cultivating the children's autonomy through peer play.

Teacher Strategies in the Play Yard

6

Credit: Lynn Bradley

T HE TEACHER OUT in the play yard has three goals. The first goal is to promote autonomous peer play, which for many children will not be that difficult. Children identify the yard as a place for play in which they, rather than the teachers, define games and themes. Many children find independent play easy and natural. However, some children, whose skills are not as accomplished yet, find play independent of the teacher a challenge. For these children, teacher intervention may be necessary.

A second goal for the teacher in the play yard is to support focused pretend play. When the first goal of autonomy has been achieved, self-directed pretend play provides an additional dimension for development. Children have a natural ability to pretend and create imaginary worlds and roles. Pretend play encourages children to think flexibly, entertain multiple perspectives, collaborate, and increase their use of language literacy skills and numeracy (Fromberg, 1999).

A third goal of the teacher in the play yard is to maintain the duration of autonomous peer play. Children are motivated to affiliate. When children pretend together in self-directed play of long duration, they will exercise demanding intellectual and social skills in creative problem solving, organizing and remembering information, and attempting to control their impulses to keep the game going.

In order to promote autonomous pretend play with peers that is focused and of long duration, teachers can adopt one of two types of strategies based on occurrences in the yard. Table 6.1 defines the two types of strategies teachers can use in the play yard to support children's autonomy. One type of strategy involves indirect coordination of ecological features through preparation and observation. The physical environment is defined by the setup and refined as children enter the ecology. A second type of strategy involves direct intervention, occurring under circumstances when play loses focus or becomes unsafe. This second type of strategy includes soliciting, verifying, and reinforcing information, or interrupting play to promote focus or to insure safety. The teacher has a choice to intervene from inside the context of the play theme or from outside the play theme. It is almost always more effective to take into account the children's play theme and intervene from inside the context of the thematic episode, as the theme is a significant feature of the ecology. Figure 6.1 presents a guide to the teacher's decision-making process during self-directed peer play and is a helpful reference throughout this chapter.

INDIRECT COORDINATION OF THE ECOLOGY

Strategies that involve daily setup activities, the provision of materials that cue for a particular play theme or interactive activity, and the definition and separation of play groups during play can be categorized as indirect coordination of the ecology. By establishing areas for play, the teacher is providing protected space where children can initiate interactions, verbally communicate needs and desires, and negotiate actions with others. The teacher observes how the children use and interpret the cues of the ecology in order to make needed refinements.

Preparation of the Ecology

Preparation precedes the presence of children playing. It is concerned with establishing the physical environment of the ecology. As explained

TABLE 6.1: Teacher Strategies to Support Children's Autonomy

	INDIRECT COORDINATION OF THE ECOLOGY	DIRECT INTERVENTION
Goals	To establish areas of play where children can initiate interactions, verbally communicate needs and desires, and negotiate actions with others	To promote focus and ensure safety
What to observe	How children use and interpret cues of the ecology	How the play episode progresses through the three points of initiation, negotiation, and enactment
When to support	Prior to and during peer play	When play loses focus and/or becomes unsafe
How to support	• Daily setup • Provision of materials • Observation • Definition and separation of play groups	• Soliciting, verifying information • Reinforcing or elaborating on information • Interrupting
Types of support	Preparation of the Ecology • Creation of space • Creation of an imaginary place Refinement of the Ecology • Localization of play groups • Separation of play groups • Reference to space • Elaboration of play theme	• Inside the context of the play theme • Outside the context of the play theme

FIGURE 6.1: A Guide to the Teacher's Decision-Making Process During Self-Directed Play

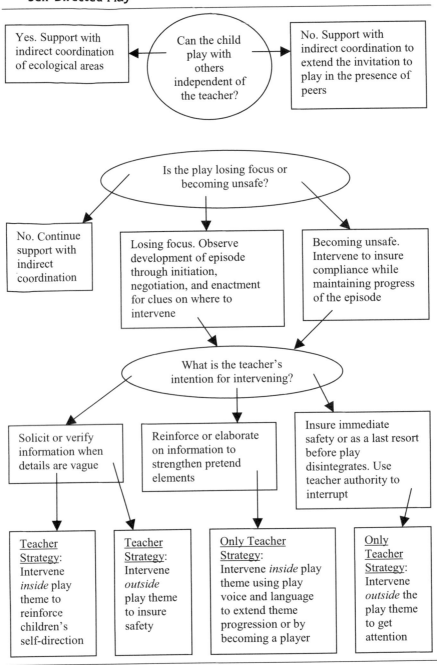

in Chapter 1, an ecology is defined as a distinct physical area in which physical and social cues are presented that direct or influence thematic play. Setup cues make evident what is to be "done" in a defined area, thereby supporting children's negotiation of a play theme. In "Making a New Road," for example, Karen's elegant setup of initial play props and easily accessible, arranged toys on an adjacent shelf offer support when the interaction begins to falter.

Preparation of the ecology begins upon entry into the area of supervision before any of the children arrive. The teacher scans the environment for appropriate and adequate "places" where groups of children can go and stay. The children's peer play is aided and facilitated by the localization of activity to particular and well-defined areas. Teacher setup activities include the arrangement of play area ecologies so that the areas will accommodate a small and manageable number of players, and, at the same time, spatially protect players from disruption by other ongoing activity in the yard.

The Creation of Space

For Karen, creation of places for the children to play involves defining "space." The sand pit, for example, is spatially arranged as two halves of a circle, with sand toys arranged in both halves. Such an arrangement is intended to accommodate comfortably two separate groups of players of between two and four players each. Refer to Figure 1.1, in Chapter 1, for an illustration of spatial preparation. The space is cued with materials that are familiar in sand play. The space is geometrically arranged so that on-looker and/or parallel play might be possible. Karen's spatial setup is designed so that less experienced or shy players are afforded the opportunity to participate in interactions without necessarily requiring refined initiating skills. This might be the case if socially adept players occupy one half of the space while a shy or less experienced child occupies the other half.

The Creation of an Imaginary Place

For Ken, creation of places for the children to play involves creating "places" that evoke pretend play. Ken piles the sand in the sand pit up into a high hill, for example, with trenches for water flow surrounding the hill's sides and shovels stuck in the hill ready for digging. From Ken's perspective, children can imagine entering an actual place, which invites interaction. In this case, the "place" includes a mountain, a valley, and, with the addition of water running from an adjacent tap, the opportunity for

rivers and dams to dig. According to Ken, a teacher's successful maintenance of the duration of a play episode is linked to the attraction or "pull"
of an interesting setup. Karen and Ken see the preparation of the outdoor
ecology as a scaffold where either space or place supports and promotes
the children's interactive play by concretely defining a specifically cued
area around which interaction will occur.

Refinement of the Ecology

Once play has begun, teacher strategies involve the refinement of ecological cues and play group locations. The teacher localizes and separates
play groups into manageable play sizes, where manageable is defined as
the group's ability to preserve cohesive interaction given the number of
players involved. Play can often break down if negotiations between
numerous players prove too complex. In the case of Matthew, Raymond,
and Lawrence, two was the maximum group size that could be sustained.
Manageable play size varies with the degree of sophistication of the players
involved. It also varies with the presence of an adult, who may be able to
preserve the interaction, but at the cost of doing the interactive work for
the children. The purpose of the teacher's actions is to accommodate the
children's developing communicative skills depending on the capacity of
the players to hold the interaction together under a variety of cognitive and
linguistic challenges.

Localization of Play Groups

This strategy is exemplified by Karen, who on one occasion, seeing a
roving band of children running frenetically in the yard, calls, "Where are
you playing?" Her question prompts the group to localize their interaction.
This localization strategy serves to place the group, thereby creating less
of a disturbance for other groups. Localization also helps the group to focus
on their own play intentions without the added cognitive and linguistic
complexity of trying to incorporate a variable setting into the content of
their play.

Separation of Play Groups

Over the course of a shared history of play, children are accustomed
to engaging in role play in predictable and specific areas of the yard. One
of the salient cues for thematic play in an ecology is the children's recollec-
tion of past thematic play there (see Figure 6.2). Teachers can refer to such

FIGURE 6.2: What Is Played Yesterday Is on Children's Minds When Next They Enter the Area

Credit: Lynn Bradley

areas to localize and separate play interactions. For example, when a group of children enter a spatially separate area where a second group is deep into a lengthy episode, Karen redirects the first group to a separate area of the yard: "You guys can have that house over there. These guys have this house now." This strategy functions both to acknowledge the ongoing play of both parties as well as to protect the play space from external disruption.

As in "Needles," there are forms of play where disruption and invasion are an integral part of the play. Lawrence's attempt to invade the diffuse play between Matthew and Raymond resulted in a more focused and creative sociodramatic form of play. While it is often difficult to determine what effect an invasion will have, the teacher must make a judgment about whether to maintain the integrity of the existing group or allow influence from the outside. In the case of the "Needles" episode, Ken delayed separation until Raymond and Matthew explicitly chose to play by themselves after previously luring Lawrence into engagement.

The intention of the separation strategy is to keep players focused on the skills of negotiation and communication without the distraction of others. To some extent such territorial invasion is allowed, however, since it provides a vivid challenge to problem-solving skills. The challenge for the teacher is in determining whether an invasion is constructive and facilitates play or destructive and disrupts play.

Reference to Space

Both teachers mention space to the children as an explanation when locating or separating play groups. Teachers refer to space in two ways: (1) by acknowledging the ongoing play episode; and (2) by acknowledging the limitation on the number of players in an ecology. An example of using space to acknowledge the play episode is when a number of children are using the sand pit. A second group of children hover quite close by, doing cartwheels in the sand. Ken redirects the second group away from the sand, giving as a reason that "these kids are trying to build things here." The purpose of Ken's redirection is to refer to the ecology as a defined place of activity. His request instructs the children to consider the perspective of others.

An example of limiting the number of players in the ecology is furnished by Ken's response to Casey's invitation to help build a dam in the sand pit. "There are just too many kids in there—there's too many kids for us to make a dam in the water." Ken's intention is to help children be aware that the number of players in a successful interaction is limited.

Elaboration of the Play Theme

Refinement also relates to how children interpret the prepared ecology once they are playing in it. The teacher can elaborate with additional props or a variation on setup to extend and prolong the interaction. This strategy remains indirect as the teacher is using cues in the physical environment to direct thematic play. Ken, for example, adds a "second dam" to the ecology as the water threatens to overwhelm the first dam, thereby extending the theme to two dams and prolonging the episode.

Protecting Ongoing Play Space

Supporting children through indirect coordination of the ecology involves protecting children's interactive space. The teacher sets up spatial areas for separate and uninterrupted play. The teacher manages the interactive flow between play spaces and play partners. The teacher informs children with explicit references to the play space that space is indeed a factor in the successful management of a play event. And the teacher uses physical cues in the ecology to extend or elaborate on self-directed themes. Under such supervision, children can learn the features of successful preparation of an area for play.

The "Making a New Road" episode is an elegant example of how Danny and Chris understand and use spatial separation themselves to successfully manage the interests of Lawrence and thereby extend the progression of the episode on several occasions. In an ideal world, the teacher would only have to observe play in the yard as it progresses purely though the interactions of the children. The teacher would offer enrichment to play yard ecologies through the preparation of the ecology. Learning is extended and challenged in enriched setups based on the teacher's observation of ecological play over time.

Often the opportunity for enrichment occurs as children are using the ecology and the teacher, by observation, can see a "next step" in the elaboration of social and intellectual skills. If the adjustment or addition to the play yard ecology is successfully incorporated into play, the next day's setup can take this "next step" into account. For example, Karen adds large blocks to a self-generated airplane game in the sand pit after hearing children comment on flight destinations. "This is San Francisco," she says, "and this is Chicago," thereby localizing the self-generated theme locations to concrete places in the ecology. On another occasion, children are digging side by side in the sand pit and one child digs up a small buried toy. Ken, hoping to promote thematic play on a joint venture, returns to the area with a box into which the children can place what he calls "treasures."

Sometimes indirect preparation and refinement of the play yard ecology is not sufficient and the teacher must intervene, because children lack the necessary judgment, language, and social skills to be self-sufficient. The most important practical function of observation is to determine whether and when teacher intervention is necessary.

DIRECT INTERVENTION IN THE PLAY EPISODE

In practice, teacher intervention is necessary. However, since one goal for the play yard is for the children to develop independent social skills through peer interaction, knowing when to intervene is a first step.

Criteria for Intervention

The teacher in the play yard offers direct intervention in pretend play with peers when the interaction loses focus due to lack of social or intellectual skills. At this point the teacher intervenes to reinvigorate the episode. Direct intervention is also needed when either physical or psychological safety is an issue. While the episode might be quite focused, player health is compromised so that immediate attention is necessary.

Children's Interaction Loses Focus

The teacher observes the progression of peer play based on the episode's development through initiation, negotiation, and enactment. These three points serve as reference markers where the teacher in the yard intervenes in order to support the continuation of peer play.

Initiation. During initiation, children are deciding with whom to play. Initiation requires that an acknowledgement for participation be received between players. If players have a history of shared play together, such acknowledgment can be quite subtle, such as a simple exchange of smiles or an idiosyncratic scream upon arrival in the yard. The teacher may decide to intervene when children are not explicitly aware that initiation, as a social act, requires acknowledgment from another. In some cases, this feature of socialization is unclear to children, as when the interests of a child who is desperately chasing after another in order to play is misinterpreted as intending harm. The teacher intervenes to slow the pace and clarify who wants to play with whom. For example, Raymond is chasing Casey.

Karen steps up to Casey, "Do you know why Raymond is chasing you?"

Casey answers, wide-eyed, "No."

"Well then ask him. Say, 'Why are you chasing me?'"

Raymond, having reached Casey, is available to listen as Casey queries him. Raymond responds, "'Cause I want to play with you."

Karen probes further, "What do you say, Casey?"

Casey looks relieved and smiles. "O.K."

Sometimes the teacher will need to intervene in unfocused play because initiation of a new member has not been clarified.

In "Needles," Ken has observed Lawrence, Raymond, and Matthew struggle over the use of the large climber. Ken queries Raymond and Matthew.

"I think Lawrence wants to play with you."

Raymond quickly reject the idea: "No!"

Matthew concurs.

"Well, you need to *tell* him that," Ken clarifies, "'cause I think he's getting confused. Sometimes he thinks you're playing with him and he's not sure." Awareness of another helps establish opportunities where children can consider the perspective of others in the yard.

Negotiation. During the negotiation phase of the play episode, children decide what they are playing. Here, too, the interaction can lose focus. The teacher decides to intervene when players are unsure about what they are doing together. Teacher intervention helps to identify the theme and affiliated roles. For example, Karen watches a group of children running back and forth in the yard repeatedly. She asks: "You guys? Wait. What's going on?" This prompts a clarification from one of the children: "Warren and Carl are the bad guys, and we don't want them to get us." At this point the teacher can decide if she is comfortable with the level and quality of the now defined activity, and, if so, support the children's play with details provided by the children's own interpretation of their actions. Intervening during the negotiation phase will stimulate planning, problem solving, and language skills.

Teachers can also identify the theme by direct involvement, as when a group of children enter the sand pit ecology and see Ken digging. "What are you doing?" one of the children asks. "I'm making Cut-Away-Mountain," Ken responds on cue. "Want to help?"

Identifying roles is another way teachers can regain focus during the negotiation phase of peer play. Pretend roles clarify what each player is doing by suggesting various expected or stereotypical activities. Workers can dig if they are building a dam, babies can crawl and perhaps cry, and by implication need someone to take care of them. Karen and Ken identify thematic roles either by asking players who they are, or, if players are quite unfocused, suggesting or assigning roles. Thus, Karen asks a girl entering the yard holding a baby and in the company of another girl, "Are you the Mommy?" The girl quickly responds: "No, we are sisters, and we are lost, and we don't have any parents." From this interchange, it becomes clear how such a question also functions to prompt the use of language. At the very least, Karen's query informs her of the children's current play theme by giving the players the opportunity to verbalize.

Explicit role assignment can be directly suggested by the teacher, for example, when Ken solicits help in making a dam: "We need some workers here!" Intervention during negotiation prompts children both to be aware of their own individual needs and desires and to extend the language skills used to express such needs.

Enactment.   During the enactment phase the play theme is expanded, developed, and/or transformed. The teacher may decide to intervene when the interaction loses focus amongst multiple player perspectives. A pretend play episode can sometimes progress in details of which not all players are aware or are perhaps not ready to accept.

One way the teacher intervenes during the progression of theme development is by providing a rich elaboration of contextual cues. During "The Dam Is Breaking," Ken finds Lawrence digging out a break in the dam. He raises his voice in a shifted register, bends forward in an alert posture, and accompanies the play voice with a "call of alarm": "Oh no! No! Block the dam! Block the dam!" Ken's verbal and nonverbal cues essentially "load" the ecological setup with information about what is to be done. Such loading of contextual cues ensures that regardless of differences in communicative skills or competencies, players will be cued to the definition of the social setting, in this case the "dam" game. By modeling both verbal and nonverbal interaction strategies, Ken shows how to inform others of play intentions during pretend.

When Ken's strategy fails to deter Lawrence, not because he is unaware of the theme but because he has a different idea, Ken structures a negotiation about the theme's elaboration by offering to Lawrence, "Say, say, 'Can we break the dam?'"

Lawrence complies: "Can we break the dam?"

"What do you guys say?" asks Ken.

"No!" says Casey quickly, since his game is to build up the dam.

The others chime in with their refusal. Rejecting requests are so tempting in the preschooler's desire for control (see Figure 6.3). Especially when permission is sought, rejecting requests can be more frequent than accepting requests. Lawrence does not have much of an advantage in swaying opinions at this point in the episode. Ken might have structured the theme's

FIGURE 6.3: The Persistent Attempt to Challenge and Gain Control Is One of Two Themes of the Preschool Peer Group.

Credit: Lynn Bradley

progression by suggesting that Lawrence ask, "Where can I break the dam?" Once power to decide is granted, children are often far more flexible than when merely asking for permission.

Safety

Physical Safety. Physical safety is an obvious occasion for intervention. Karen intervenes frequently in this regard. When Warren is climbing up the large climber with a stuffed kitty in one hand, Karen comments, "It's not safe to climb with a kitty in your hand. Your hand might slip." On another occasion Karen reminds a child up in the climber about a yard rule: "Blankets can't go up there. It's not safe." These two examples show how demanding play yard ecologies can be. Without the use of dramatic props because they would interfere with safe climbing, children are required to imagine without material cues. Karen refers to safety by using short directives, which are almost always complied with by the targeted child without disruption to the episode. Compliance does not generally surface as an issue between Karen and the children, due in part to her use of comments rather than commands. She couples her comments with safety explanations to justify her requests for compliance.

Karen intervenes more directly in "Two Guys." To reduce the risk of injury, Karen discourages running, and does so with Lawrence, using the added explanation, "I told Lawrence that if he wanted to play with you he should play with you and not chase you. O.K.?" She then adds a cautionary threat: "'Cause somebody will end up in trouble for running and then they'll have to go inside." Karen establishes a rule for the incentive to play together.

On another occasion reported in "Two Guys," when Warren participates in an action that is strictly unacceptable, Karen again couples her request with a cautionary threat intended to highlight the significance of his actions: "Warren, that's not safe. Don't push kids on the slide or you'll have to get off." Physical safety is a predominant feature when supervising play in the yard. Like Karen, who uses short directives often accompanied with a brief explanatory comment, the teacher develops effective ways to insure compliance while still maintaining the progress of the episode.

Psychological Safety. Psychological safety is another occasion for intervention. Psychological safety issues arise during taunting or rejection. Recall Raymond and Matthew rejecting Lawrence in "Needles." Raymond's rejection of Lawrence must be psychologically painful despite Lawrence's persistent return to the ecology. Here surfaces a conflict of teacher goals. On the one hand, Raymond and Matthew's exclusion of Lawrence is an occasion when intervention for safety is needed. On the other hand, Raymond and Matthew had created an alliance and shifted from undirected to sociodramatic play, albeit by exclusion. Gallas (1998) describes the sometimes raw relationships among children, behaviors that can be disturbing when one child intentionally isolates another or when children join together to isolate another. The responsibility of the teacher is to redress this raw behavior.

In "Needles," Ken intervenes by helping Raymond and Matthew to see that Lawrence is affected by their taunting and exclusion. Ken first identifies Lawrence's feelings as he looks at the "needle."

"That's really scary. He really believes its real, Lawrence does." Ken then gives Raymond and Matthew a way to save face, by noting the imaginary quality of the game.

"I know it's pretend. But you need to tell him that, because he thinks it's real." Ken acknowledges Raymond and Matthew's game, but also helps Raymond respond to Lawrence's distress. Ken then surfaces the implicit conflict of perspectives. Lawrence wants to play with Raymond and Matthew, and Raymond and Matthew do not want him to. What Ken does not address is Raymond and Matthew's choice of a game. They find that excluding Lawrence is far more engaging and stimulating than creating their own independent scenario. Their exploration of themes of power and control are experienced at the expense of Lawrence. While preschool play can be quite raw and primitive, and exploration of power and control makes sense from a developmental perspective, such interactions are an opportunity for learning about how people treat each other. Taunting and excluding, like physical aggression, are not acceptable. Just as preschool children learn to verbalize their needs and desires rather than act them out in a physically aggressive manner, so too, preschool children can learn conventions that negotiate psychological needs and desires rather than excluding another.

As a first step, respectful conventions during play can be quite rudimentary. Raymond could have been coached to say, "I'm playing with Matthew right now. I'll let you know when I'm done." Oftentimes this simple negotiation will give the persistent intruder the permission to leave, as the game no longer is one of power and control. Raymond and Matthew could have also been directed to "play your own game. Kids don't play the 'You Can't Come Up Here' game at this school. It hurts people's feelings." Just as Karen admonishes a gun-toting play group with, "You're not gonna shoot. It scares kids and I don't like it," exclusion can be treated in the same manner. Of course, telling children what not to do is not as helpful as offering them alternatives to do. With Lawrence's departure after Raymond and Matthew refuse to play with him, Ken might have suggested an elaboration on the needle theme, which could have engaged them both without the need of an external source. More than likely the two would have reverted to gazing about the yard and commenting on birdies.

Often exclusion is cut to the quick when children are asked whom they are playing with. Either the excluded child is not mentioned, and the teacher can refocus the group in a separate and defined area, or the excluded child is mentioned and can be asked if she or he wants to play the "You Can't Come Up Here" game, for example. Because of children's interest during the preschool years in power and control, exclusion as a method of interactive play can be expected. The teacher in the yard will be most effective in helping children make sense of the themes of power and control by highlighting options where children can feel powerful in the imaginative world without needing to isolate others.

In summary, as teachers observe peer interactions from the three-point framework of initiation, negotiation, or enactment, they understand where in the progression of the episode the children can use support. Teachers also monitor for physical and psychological safety. Such support is provided by the teacher's modeling language skills, stimulating children to consider their own and others' perspective, facilitating flexibility in thinking, and helping the children to integrate shifts from reality to fantasy.

Types of Intervention

When the episode has lost focus, or when physical or psychological safety is compromised, the teacher in the play yard has a choice of intervention strategies. The intent of the intervention will determine which strategy the teacher will use. The teacher might need to solicit or verify information when details of the play episode are vague. The teacher might decide to reinforce or elaborate on information to strengthen the meaning of pretend elements as the episode progresses. The teacher might also choose to use her status as an authority figure to comment on an episode's interruption or to interrupt an episode to insure safety.

In all play yard intervention, the teacher acknowledges the perspective of the children playing precisely because the children are establishing the thematic cues for the ecology in each episode. Acknowledging the perspective of the child in pretend play helps to substantiate the separate identity of the child. In this sense, acknowledgment is functioning to promote the child's emerging self-concept. Berit Bae (1987), a Swedish educator, describes how the strategy of acknowledgment accomplishes such support for the development of self-concept:

> When I acknowledge you, I see you as a separate individual with an identity and integrity of your own. I bestow on you the rights to your own experiences. I might not agree or approve of them, but I grant you the right to have them anyway . . . I see you as an expert of your own experience. (p. 9)

Attending to the perspective of the child is an especially powerful tool for the teacher in the play yard. Such acknowledgment confers credibility, validity, and respect not only to the play event, which *is* the current reality in the ecology, but also to the perspective of the child within such a reality.

In considering when and for what reason to intervene, the teacher decides in which context they wish to interact. There are two contexts in which the teacher can intervene: (1) from *inside* the theme of the play episode; and (2) from *outside* the context of the play theme. Intervening from inside the play theme reinforces the children's ability to model social interaction with peers through imaginative, self-generated scenarios. By staying inside the play theme, the teacher keeps the direction of the episode in the hands of the children. Intervening from inside the play theme maintains the integrity of the theme. The teacher presents less of a disruption upon intervention and thus supports self-directed interactive play of longer duration. In a sense, intervening from inside the play theme disguises the teacher as a nonintrusive player. Addressing the play theme as if it were real is particularly effective as a tool in promoting autonomous, imaginative play of long duration. In terms of achieving the goals of the play yard, this is the optimal strategy.

There are considerations that override the goals of maintaining autonomous, self-directed pretend play with peers. Intervening from outside the context of the play theme will highlight the teacher's role as an authority figure. In circumstances of safety, or when the episode already appears to be breaking down due to loss of focus, teacher authority can be an effective tool to address compromised integrity in the episode. Interrupting the episode is therefore one type of intervention that will always be outside the play theme.

Interventions That Solicit or Verify Information

When in doubt about the focus of an episode of pretend play in the yard, the teacher can solicit or verify information. Collecting thematically cued information is crucial in the yard because themes are often child-generated. A teacher will need to solicit information to determine whether children are making the distinction between real and pretend. One good way to find out is to ask, as Karen does. Having observed Carl throw Warren to the ground, Karen asks, "Are you guys really fighting, or are you just pretending?" Having heard an explanation from Carl, Karen refers to the interaction with an acknowledgment and clarification of Warren's feelings: "Warren, are you still angry at Carl?" In this episode, Karen's queries for further information promote elaboration. During the screening of this episode, Karen explains her intentions in adopting this strategy:

> I don't know this for a fact, but there may be a part of me that is always aware . . . that *I'm not sure* what just happened, and I don't want to be jumping on kids or blaming kids for something that they weren't responsible for. So, . . . there was a lot that I missed, that I see now in the tape, or that I didn't see when I was out

there . . . I can't say for sure, but that may be why I rarely step in
and go, "This is it," or "You have to go in," unless I've been aware
of everything that just took place.

Although Karen's prompting for clarification is based on her own need for
further information, it nevertheless stimulates both complex perspective
taking and the language skills necessary to express such perspectives.
Karen's intervention is one that occurs from outside the pretend theme.
While she has interrupted the interactive flow, her tentative demeanor of
curiosity allows Carl to explain the circumstances sufficiently for Karen to
feel assured that the issue of safety has been resolved and for Carl to quickly
return to play.

The teacher may intervene to solicit or verify information for professional curiosity. Teachers may want to hear players articulate their understanding of the episode to get a sample of verbal and cognitive skills. A
group of boys outfitted in handmade masks and power arm bands are
darting in and out of other children's play spaces, creating loud and disgruntled cries for the teacher. Karen approaches the boys, asking: "Who's
the boss here?" which surfaces a group spokesperson: "I am. I'm the black
Power Ranger!" As an intervention strategy, regardless of whether a spokesperson actually exists, the question is intended to reveal the group's intentions in such disruptive running. Karen quizzes the Power Ranger on what
they are doing. Karen's intervention occurs from inside the pretend theme,
by addressing the child in the imaginary role. Upon further observation,
the teacher might consider whether the group as currently defined is too
large for the children to manage independent of the disruption of others.
Further questioning might reveal whether the group has a reason for running pell-mell into other play groups or whether the group would be better
served by focusing attention on a specific area, once localized.

Intervening from inside the play theme to solicit or verify information
can involve addressing the children in their pretend role. Karen, verifying
a presumption from previous play, asks a crawling child, "Are you a kitty
now?" Her question prompts the kitty to respond, "Meow. I want milk."
Karen's question allows the kitty to elaborate on the play theme. On another
occasion, as Ken is digging with others at Cut-Away-Mountain, he refers
to the obvious bulge of a telephone receiver, which is snug and tight in the
pants of a child digging alongside him: "Why do you have that there?" And
when Ken later sees another player frantically chopping at the mountain,
he asks, "What are you doing, trying to knock down the mountain?" In all
these examples, the teacher's questioning prompted some form of thematic
elaboration from the addressed player. Intervention from inside the play
theme to verify or elaborate on information stimulates coherent thinking

by prompting children to make attributions about their actions. As with all questions and comments made by the teacher from inside the context of the play episode, dialogue provides a model for possible discourse strategies by the children in future play activities.

Interventions That Reinforce and Elaborate on Information

Reinforcing or elaborating on information in a peer play episode is a particularly effective strategy when out in the play yard. Children are often creating their own scenarios in flexible ecologies. A climbing apparatus or a sand area can support any number of imaginary themes with any number of associated roles. Ken's elaboration of contextual cues in "The Dam Is Breaking!" is a good example of how a teacher reinforces the information in an episode. Ken provides multiple verbal and nonverbal cues that highlight significant events, better assuring that players will remain aware of the episode's progress. He calls out "Oh, no!" and laughs as a punctuation when the dam breaks. Ken uses labeling to reinforce episodic events, as well as to elaborate an opening for future verbal exchanges between players. For example, Ken observes two areas where water is collecting: "Oh. You made a double dam." Reinforcing events in the episode serves as a model in the use of language to inform others.

Ken adds thematic details as a "next step" elaboration for the children who up until now were gathered to contain the water. "This'll be where the lake is. Right here. When you make a dam, you have to make a place for the water to store up. Like a lake, or a reservoir." Now the children have a reason to keep on interacting, this time to maintain the lake that catches the water whenever a dam might break. Ken extends the episode's duration in "The Dam Is Breaking" by intervening from inside the context of the play theme to both reinforce and elaborate.

Ken also reinforces and elaborates on information by becoming a player in "The Dam Is Breaking." Ken intervenes from inside the play theme as a player, adopting a play voice tone and/or rhythm, using commentary coincident with actions or events in the episode, and using stereotypic gestures and postures in regard to the children's pretend theme. As a modeling device for interactive competency, Ken is providing strategies that children can use on their own to integrate interactions. He yells out in mock emergency: "Flash flood! Flash flood! Look out below! Look out below in the valley!" As he moves into the ecology with a large shovel, he explains as he digs, "I'm going to dig out this channel because I want the river to flow here." Ken's use of commentary functions to help children learn to interpret the circumstances of their game. Ken adopts stereotyped gestures and postures to add an overlay of additional reinforcement for theme development. He stands rigidly to one side of a dam break. He squats down to signal special attention during buildup.

The teacher can reinforce information in the episode by addressing the child in the pretend role, as when a child crawls past Karen and meows. Karen simply comments: "Hi, Kitty." The teacher can make a passing comment that refers to thematic content, as when Ken walks by a large block construction and says, "That's a powerful spaceship." The teacher can also reinforce thematic content for players outside the episode, as when a group of children enter an already occupied ecology and Karen intervenes with the information, "That's their refrigerator." Reinforcing and elaborating acknowledges the experience of the child and helps to confirm the child's credibility as a separate individual.

Interventions That Interrupt the Episode

There are occasions where the play episode must be interrupted by the teacher's intervention as an authority figure. All the examples offered in the section on safety fall under this type of intervention. Additionally, the episode may be disintegrating due to loss of focus or discrepant player intentions. As an example, Karen, having observed Lawrence run in and out of a play area numerous times, hopes to encourage a more integrated role for him by commenting to the play group, "Lawrence doesn't understand this game." In an early phase of "The Dam Is Breaking," Ken prompts Robert to explain his play intentions with the directive: "Tell him what you're doing, Robert!" Ken interrupts to encourage a negotiation of player needs so that the episode will continue. Following Ken's prompt for definition, Robert and Casey exchange information that elaborates the episode into a damming game. In "Needles," Ken's interruption to prompt Raymond to clarify the pretend nature of his play for Lawrence is successful because Ken affords respect and credibility to Raymond's imaginary play theme and to Lawrence's feelings. As a result, Lawrence chooses a new ecology, and Raymond and Matthew are left to experience social interaction based on their own devices.

Intervention can also occur when a child interrupts the episode to bring a possible misdeed of another player to the attention of the teacher. Karen responds by stating that the meaning of the misdeed "depends on why he did it." Karen is interested in the reasons for the behavior rather than in responding directly to how the behavior was delivered. On another occasion, when a child is running with gleeful delight away from the threat of being kissed, and the kissing girl wonders about her friend's inclinations, Ken responds, "I don't know if he wants you to kiss him or not. I can't tell." In regards to a sand-throwing incident that occurs in front of Ken as he stands observing, he asks, "Do you want me to see you do that?" Nearly always, the occasion for interruption serves as a point of reflection of player perspective.

The strategies identified in this chapter highlight a significant feature of teaching in the play yard. Teaching in the play yard is a mutual effort between the children and the teachers to support learning through interactive play. Based on the teacher's knowledge of the children's past history of play, ecologies promote independent interpretation from each child's interests, level of development, and competence. The teacher becomes the guide, attending to new or idiosyncratic features of the children's play and helping to support each child's appreciation of his or her own unique role in the play experience. Learning unfolds with the children's interpretation and enactment of the cues of the ecological areas, including those cues offered in the moment from the children's imagination. The overriding goal of teachers in the play yard is to promote and protect the interactive work experienced by the children in play. As such, the play yard, with its open space, its leniency in noise requirements, and its flexibility for innovative interpretation of area cues, offers children a wide berth to practice emerging socialization skills. The outdoor teaching strategies identified in this chapter give teachers a way both to observe emerging social interaction skills during play and to converse with players, while honoring the children's autonomous pace and mode of activity.

The Social and Cultural Organization of the Play Yard

7

Credit: Bob Devaney

THIS CHAPTER ANALYZES outdoor classroom events in terms of the implications such events have for two teachers and one group of children in an early childhood classroom. In the analysis of the four peer play episodes in Chapters 2 through 5, a number of interactive peer practices and routines were identified. Episodes of play are often initiated by requesting an acknowledgment of affiliation: "We're friends, right?" Requests for play can frequently be met by resistance, however, establishing a precedent for vigilance if play with others is desired. Termination of a play episode frequently occurs without warning or recognition, leaving a playmate unpredictably without a partner. Such vigilance and unpredictability together create a quality of fragility to peer interactions.

Children respond with play routines intended to assure participation and some measure of control. The introduction of a new play idea into an on-going event involves securing an agreement from companions in order to incorporate the new theme into the action. Children use a change in voice tone to signal or mark a shift in theme and use register differences to indicate different roles. Highly ritualized and repetitive behavior like screaming, dangling, running, and feigned aggression and fear emerge when language skills are not accessible or available, under new circumstances, or when a playmate is shy or feeling threatened by a challenge such as the entrance of another playmate. These practices and routines make up what is called the social and cultural organization of the classroom—a kind of social etiquette that tells children and teachers what is O.K. and what is not O.K. to do in the classroom. The social and cultural organization of the classroom can be either conscious or not so conscious. This chapter summarizes the information in previous chapters by identifying (1) peer routines that have a shared history and meaning to this group of children, and (2) practices in the play yard that define the teacher's expectations for appropriate behavior. Understanding the play yard culture is important to teachers, administrators, and policy makers in early childhood education who are interested in explicitly incorporating autonomous outdoor play activities into a curriculum for the development of socialization.

PLAY ROUTINES SERVING THE PEER CULTURE

One premise of my research is that play yard events are embedded in an interactive teaching-learning process that occurs within the context of the children's own world and peer culture. Children construct repertoires of communication skills needed to negotiate their interests. While the peer culture certainly is influenced by the adult world, children nonetheless produce actions that refer to some shared notions regarding their own private world of fantasy, friendships, ceremony, and etiquette. Such actions are important for the teacher in the play yard to understand because they occur so frequently. For example, allegiances are jockeyed about even in the midst of an episode, the emotional tug of a single partner becomes a primary focus of attention compared to the challenge of sharing partnerships. Fantasy themes spring forth simply by being up in a climbing apparatus. Voices loudly enrich a game's progress with sound effects, poetry, and song. Initiation and theme elaborations require acknowledgment, establishing a precedence for repeated requests: "O.K.? O.K.?" "O.K."

In this section, I first outline the characteristics of a play routine, then I identify three examples of peer play routines from the anecdotal episodes and discuss their meaning and function with respect to the peer culture. My assumption here is that the peer culture exists in all classrooms. It has particular scope for expression in the play yard. To the extent that teachers are familiar with and understand the nature of such an organized system, teachers can better guide the development of socialization from the perspective of the child's own world and culture.

Characteristics of a Peer Play Routine

A peer play routine can be characterized according to its observable features as well as with regard to the function it serves in the peer culture.

Observable Features

William Corsaro (1986) identifies three features of a peer play routine. All three are vividly recognizable. In this discussion I elaborate on Corsaro's research.

First, the play routine is enacted with others *mutually*. Children want to be affiliated with each other. Often, but not always, children will express pleasure and excitement as they engage in such an activity by laughing and shrieking. One example of this kind of routine is the combined running and chasing activity that children regularly engage in when the setting allows. The routine is triggered by one child running away from one or more others, while regularly looking back to keep in eye contact with the others. This initial action prompts chasing by those left behind, whereupon the routine is fully enacted in a combined chasing game, which includes regular eye contact, smiling, and/or laughing. The poignancy of such an activity is the routine's mutuality.

A second feature of all play routines is the *highly ritualized* nature of the enacted activity. Movements occur in a readily identifiable fashion to all children. Such ritualization of movement serves to trigger the initiation of the routine easily without any need of negotiation. In the example of the chasing routine, the beginning of the activity is initiated simply by the signal of one child running from and looking back at another. Dora's "fallen" pose is another example of a highly ritualized routine where the stereotypical fallen gesture communicates a need for care without any words having been spoken.

In addition to being ritualized, the actions of a peer play routine are also *repetitive*. It is the repetitive nature of the play routine that makes such a peer activity immediately distinctive and recognizable to observers. The combined ritualized and repetitive actions of the routine make it a highly predictable activity.

A fourth feature of peer play routines is that the activity is *adaptable*. It is not specifically dependent on any one locale or set of players. The chasing routine can be enacted anywhere when one child initiates the trigger of running-and-looking-back and at least one other child follows up with the chase. Some routines are also adaptable to almost any social situation. These routines are quite powerful because they can be enacted by children with no previous history of shared play experience. The running routine is just such a universal routine. Other routines are much more private to children, with the triggering mechanism evoking something based on the shared history of the players. The private routines retain the feature of adaptability, since they are readily initiated in any setting.

Function of a Play Routine

The function of a play routine in the peer culture is to secure or confirm bonding between participants. When it is acted out, a routine is extremely powerful in acknowledging participation among children. It is a means by which children are able to relate immediately with another without need for language or negotiation. It is therefore an activity that can be adopted and relied upon when language skills are not available or accessible. In its ease and immediacy of initiation, a peer play routine can also function to quickly reconfirm the mutuality of a shared relationship. One sees the chasing routine, for example, being adopted in circumstances where children are new and/or shy with each other, or in cases where children do not share the same language, or when the ecology is impoverished. One also notes the chasing routine adopted under circumstances of tenuousness, when the interactive integrity of a partnership between players is for any reason weakened or threatened. Here, the ongoing function of a routine in the peer culture is most clearly seen as a substantiation of bonds within the peer group.

The four peer play episodes detailed in the preceding chapters include a number of routines, three examples of which will now be explored. In this discussion, it will be evident that the features of a routine are mutual, ritualized, repetitive, and adaptable. Each routine will also be discussed in terms of the specific function it serves for the children in the episode.

The Danger Routine

This routine, enacted by Carl and Warren in "Two Guys," is perhaps the most vivid routine identified. At the same time, it is a perplexing activity for teachers to supervise. While Carl and Warren's game certainly serves some function in terms of affiliation, its nature as a loud, repetitive, and persistent activity puzzled us all in my classroom as we observed its repetition day after day. Prior to the discovery of Carl and Warren's use of a play routine to structure their interactive activity, this is how I described my bewilderment in my journal:

> They are distinctive in that they appear to carry their play from area to area without disruption from the varying area-specific features. That is, they have no trouble maintaining their mutual play themes independent of physical cues. This suggests a fairly complex level of cognitive or transformational ability. These two players, however, choose often to use sounds, single word utterances, and what might be described as stereotyped phrases like those in a cartoon. The point here is that while the language between these two players does not appear to be very advanced, these players are doing something to hold their play together for long stretches of time AND across different areas.

Observable Features

Warren and Carl's actions can now be interpreted in terms of the various features of a play routine. First, a number of actions that are mutual in fashion are enacted. The referents "Guy" and "Ahhh!" are specifically used by both Warren and Carl to signal the mutually shared activity. The enactment of the activity also involves mutual side-by-side dangling from the surface of the slide, face-to-face engagement in caught glances, and grabbing for one another. All such actions act to signal or promote a mutual context to the activity. Verbal references to this mutuality are also involved, such as this sequence:

> Warren yells a request to Carl. "Arh! Gimme!"
> Carl grabs for Warren's hand, switching back to the role referent. "Guy, what? Got you!"

The activity is also highly ritualized. The act of hanging precariously on the surface of the slide, accompanied by a yell, is readily identified as a signal to initiate the routine. The activity is also quite repetitive. It involves dangling on some spot on the slide, securing the participation of the other with an exchange of yells, and sliding down, hanging off, or pulling up from the precarious position in synch with the partner, or a combination of these actions.

As noted in the above excerpted description of Warren and Carl's play action, the activity is also quite adaptable to any setting. In fact, on a latter portion of the videotape for that day, Warren and Carl play on the tire swing. Their actions on the swing reproduce almost exactly their play on the slide. Without any prior negotiation, they both yell to each other repeatedly as they hang precariously off the spinning tire. They suggest in the tightly ritualized nature of their actions that here, too, danger is an ever-present scenario. The routine is not, however, successfully adapted to social contexts other than that between Carl and Warren, as evidenced by the misunderstanding developed between Dora and Warren. When Dora inadvertently adopts an action that triggers the danger routine for Warren, he immediately responds within the routine's ritualized structure without feeling any apparent need to explain or negotiate his actions. The routine breaks down with Dora's unwillingness to participate.

Function of the Peer Play Routine

The function of this peer play routine becomes evident upon inspection of the circumstances in which it is initiated. The first initiation and enactment of the routine occur after Warren and Carl have a "big fight." Carl returns up the slide to Warren as Warren slides down to meet Carl, and they struggle, with accompanying grunts, yells, and an acknowledging "Guy." They jointly return up the incline of the slide. The next time, the routine is initiated by Carl upon the entrance of Lawrence as a third party. The routine successfully draws Warren away from Lawrence and back into the mutual activity he shares with Carl. Carl initiates the routine a third time as Warren begins to initiate dialogue with Dora, and again Carl's initiatory yellings draw Warren back into the danger routine. The ease and immediacy of initiation in this routine functions to reconfirm the bond between Warren and Carl during points in the episode when such mutuality appears to be threatened. As a routine, it also functions to bind these two players together when their language and/or negotiating skills may not have sufficed, as indicated by the scarcity of language and negotiation during their "big fight." With these two close friends, explicit language has given way to a variety of subtle symbolic cues.

The Approach-and-Flee Peer Play Routine, I

This second example, characterized by an episodic back-and-forth quality as described by Fromberg (1999), occurs in "Needles." Raymond and Matthew play the role of threatening agents to Lawrence's advances.

Lawrence repeatedly approaches, despite threats. Characteristic of this type of chase routine, the roles switch throughout enactment, so that Lawrence's alignment with Ken also becomes the threat to Raymond and Matthew, who display typical "feigned fear" and avoidance. Corsaro (1986) has described the development of the approach-and-avoidance routine in terms of three phases: an early identification phase, which frames action in a danger or threat theme; an approach phase, which involves the cautious advance upon the threatening agent; and a final avoidance phase, which begins with the retaliatory gestures of the dangerous agent followed by the flight of the advancers. In "Needles," the approach-and-flee routine is initiated by Raymond's aggressive gestures toward Lawrence's first entrance. Lawrence's return signals the approach phase, which is followed up by Raymond, who throws a paper cup in Lawrence's direction, initiating Lawrence's flight. Lawrence's appeal to an authority figure triggers another initiation of the routine, with Raymond and Matthew fleeing. The routine is repeated numerous times. There is the addition of a "needle" to the initiation phase midway through the episode, the added retaliatory power of bullets during the avoidance phase, and the frenetic reaction by Raymond and Matthew to Ken's approach.

Observable Features

The mutuality of this activity shared by Lawrence, Raymond, and Matthew is indicated whenever the enactment of the routine breaks down. Paradoxically, the mutuality seems to be accomplished by Raymond and Matthew's exclusion of Lawrence. As a dynamic, it is accurate to say that Raymond and Matthew's mutuality is based on the active exclusion of Lawrence, though Lawrence plays a necessary role in the enactment of the routine between these three players. As soon as the exclusion of Lawrence dissipates, the mutuality breaks down. While Lawrence is necessary to the mutuality, he doesn't participate in it. His appeal to Ken indicates that he is an unwilling participant in his role in the routine. Thus, while it appears that Matthew and Raymond are involved in a separate, individual episode at times, the cohesive integrity of the play theme is intimately tied to Lawrence's attempts at entrance. When Lawrence retreats, the theme of Matthew and Raymond's activity correspondingly breaks down. When Ken points out to Lawrence that he has a choice as to whether or not to remain in repetitive interactions with Raymond, Lawrence persists in his advances. Mutuality is expressed in other ways as well. This mutuality between Matthew and Raymond is often triggered by the various signals that Matthew uses to mark jointly shared action, such as "Let's hide," "Hurry!", and "Let's go."

Function of the Peer Play Routine

For Raymond and Matthew, the function of this peer play routine is to secure a bond under circumstances of tenuousness, since the partnership between these two relatively shy boys is not firmly assured at the beginning of the episode. Lawrence, as was also evidenced in the "Making a New Road" episode, is in a phase of interaction with others where he repeatedly practices initiation in already ongoing activity but is less inclined to participate in the actual enactment of interactive play independent of a teacher. For Lawrence, the approach-and-flee routine functions to provide repeated experience in attempts at initiation of peer interaction. The routine in this example provides him with repeated experience with rejection as well. While Lawrence is experimenting with the effects of his actions on others, it is the teacher's job to look to the balance of his behavior and its consequences. One would like Lawrence's learning to be founded in accommodating consequences, as Danny, Seth, and Chris offer in "Making a New Road." Corsaro (1985) argues that in approach-and-flee routines, children attempt to gain control over the fears, concerns, and curiosities of their everyday lives. Raymond and Matthew's actions are an attempt to experience strength and fortitude within the hierarchy of the peer group, and Lawrence's actions are an attempt to gain control over peer-peer interchange for a child intellectually advanced who nonetheless is socially awkward. In terms of the approach-and-flee routines in the play yard, the teacher will be regularly balancing the advantages of alliance with the disadvantages of exclusion.

The Approach-and-Flee Peer Play Routine, II

This third example is another approach-and-flee peer play routine. It occurs in the "Making a New Road" episode when Chris nonchalantly comments to Danny and Seth: "The movie camera." These three boys had maintained an active avoidance of playing within range of either the camera or the camera technicians throughout the 3 weeks of taping. So vociferous were their activities in this regard that the head teacher and I felt compelled to deal explicitly with what appeared to be obtrusiveness on the part of the research equipment. The head teacher gave the boys a guided tour of all the equipment setup facilities. I spoke directly to both teachers about my concerns of obtrusiveness, with the hope that teachers might allay the preoccupation of these children. What happened, in fact, was that the boys incorporated their preoccupation into their peer play theme.

The boys did not appear frightened by their awareness of the camera, but rather used the presence of the equipment to promote a stereotyped flee action, coupled with shouts of "Wha-, wha-, wha-whooooooooa!" The boys' reaction is an attempt to gain control over the novelty of my unfamiliar filming equipment. Characteristic of the peer culture, such curiosity becomes readily embedded into peer play.

Observable Features

Like the other routines, this approach and flee activity is also mutually shared. In the midst of play together on the tire swing, or running pell-mell through the yard, one of the three friends notices the camera. Immediately all three flee together. The action of running appears to help solidify their mutuality.

The flee response is quite ritualized. It includes yells and exaggerated facial expressions of surprise, including raised eyebrows and wide, rounded and opened mouths in reaction to the camera. Further, fleeing often involves repetitive running in circles before the eventual and final flight out of the area. Finally, the activity is quite adaptable, as it occurs whenever and wherever they notice the camera.

Function of the Peer Play Routine

The function of this peer play routine is to serve as a means for these three children to gain control over concerns produced by the introduction of camera equipment into the setting. It is interesting to note when this routine gets triggered in the "Making a New Road" episode. It is initiated by Chris just at a point of tentative alliance between Danny, with whom Chris has up until now enjoyed almost exclusive attention, and Seth, who has been attempting entrance into the dyad:

> Danny then turns to Seth and laughs again. Chris looks up and notices the video camera. "The movie camera," he remarks casually. It is interesting at this point of alliance between Seth and Danny that Chris finds a situation for interruption. "The movie camera?" asks Danny. He looks up, sees the camera, and quickly scrambles up and abandons the play site. As he runs, Danny is looking back at the camera. Chris and Seth follow, dropping their toys and keeping their eyes fixed on Danny. Danny stops mid-yard. The three gather together outside the sand pit, looking to each other. Danny notices that the camera appears to be pointing away from their play spot. Danny returns to the sand, with Chris and Seth following. All three scramble for their abandoned toys.

The consequence of Chris's signal, "the movie camera," is that this new dyadic alliance between Danny and Seth is broken as all three scatter from the camera's view. Danny halts the full enactment of the routine, however, and presents an opportunity for the friends to return to their play activities. Now the function for Chris in triggering the routine is evident. Chris has reestablished his alliance with Danny, albeit alongside Seth, and supplanted the topic of the camera. The enactment of a routine has occurred under circumstances of tenuousness, when the interactive integrity of a partnership felt fragile.

Supervising the Peer Play Routine

The importance to teachers in understanding and identifying the peer play routine and its enactment is that decisions on play yard teaching strategies can best be made when teachers appreciate the reasons why children in a flexible space are participating in repetitive, ritualized, and sometimes unsafe activity. The strategies identified in Chapter 6 which highlight teacher negotiation from the child's perspective are most relevant here.

Routine enactment surfaces when there is a need for cohesion. In "Two Guys," the danger-and-rescue routine of dangling and hollering from the slide is a game Carl and Warren play repeatedly to assure interactive focus. Warren is ready to accept additional players into the routine. Carl is not. In "Needles," Raymond and Matthew are not cognitively prepared to enact their own imagined theme. The enactment of the approach-and-flee routine, involving being naughty, taunting Lawrence, and fleeing from Lawrence and Ken as "the teacher," integrates the content of their play in a way that they were unable to muster by themselves. Lawrence, however, wants a playmate in the routine "Needles." While he is not comfortable with the threatening tone of the routine, he continues to participate because he desires the interactive affiliation. In "Making a New Road," Chris casually announces the movie camera, thus initiating the approach-and-flee routine when his dyadic alliance with Danny is challenged by Seth's renewed participation.

In each of these routines, entry by another playmate features prominently. Most chase games outside will involve some form of entry attempt. With less experienced players, entry may be interpreted by others as a threat to be repetitively avoided. In more experienced players, children will take turns attempting entry and refusing participation by switching approach and avoidance roles. Repetitive, ritualized, and often fast-paced routine enactment serves an important integrating function for those involved. The enactment of routines in the peer group cements play interactions either when players are seeking out more experience and skills in group interaction or when the play theme is weak, threatened, or unstable.

By appreciating the peer play routine as an integrating feature in the peer group, teachers can meet children's need for involvement by offering alternatives. They can interpret the underlying motive: "I think he wants to play with you." They can facilitate entry by suggesting a new role: "Here comes a visitor. Where is the doorbell?" They can offer ideas for theme development to include an additional player: "Do you have any tea for your visitor?" Or they can arrange ecological space so that the play group can separate into more manageable sizes. Just how teachers understand peer group dynamics depends on the culture or tone of the yard as reflected in play yard expectations for valued behavior.

THE TEACHER CULTURE AND EXPECTATIONS FOR VALUED BEHAVIOR

The social and cultural organization of the play yard is defined by the interactions of the teachers and children during peer play. Teachers in the play yard value and encourage pretend play with peers because such play influences social competence. The "master players" documented by Reynolds and Jones (1997) and Fein (1985) are characterized by Fromberg (1999) as having fluidity, flexibility, and effectively rich interactions that include challenges and risk taking. Pellegrini and Smith (1998) suggest that the length of vigorous play relates to children's ability to encode and decode information in their environment (see also, Carson, Burks, & Parke, 1993; Parke, Cassidy, Burks, Carson, & Boyum, 1992). Pellegrini (1993) has found that the kind of vigorous play exemplified by Warren and Carl correlates with social problem-solving flexibility. Vigorous, imaginative play supports fluency and creativity (see Figure 7.1). Autonomous peer play in the yard is a manifestation of the peer culture, which so esteems allegiance and control but also defines the expectations of the teacher culture. Teachers in my study convey value to peer play in three ways: (1) by granting children the opportunity to possess space and materials, (2) by granting children the opportunity to choose playmates, and (3) by framing children's choice of appropriate behavior as "play."

Possession of Space and Materials

One opportunity for a child involved in pretend play with others is the possession of a play space in the school yard, including toys and other play materials, for the duration of the peer play episode. Facilities at the

FIGURE 7.1: Fluency and Creativity Are Supported Through the Children's Vigorous, Imaginative Play.

Credit: Lynn Bradley

school are generally "for everybody," and materials and toys are to be shared equally. When children are involved in a play episode, however, others wanting to use the area are redirected. Thus, esteemed objects and areas can be possessed by a group of children, with the apparent acceptance of disenfranchised others. As an example, two children have been playing dinosaurs on the large climber when two others jump up onto the climber in order to slide down the slide. Karen, hearing the disgruntled cries of the dinosaurs, informs the invaders that the others "are playing there now" and that the second group can use "that house over there," pointing to another structure. The second group readily runs to their newfound home.

Choice of Playmates

A second manifestation of the esteem bestowed on pretend play with peers by the teacher culture is the opportunity for children to be able to choose playmates. Any child already playing, or any child ready or willing to play, is given the right to accept or reject playmates. Such a privilege is extremely powerful in the peer culture, which so prizes friendship as its major bargaining chip for access into groups and possession of desired goods. Recognition of playmate choice does not mean that teachers refrain from initiating entry attempts in support of less experienced players. Karen and Ken both promote flexible thinking and perspective-taking by interpreting motives, as when Karen queries, "Lawrence wants to play with you. What can he be in your game?" or when Ken attempts to initiate a new player into the group by simultaneously offering the integrity of the group and furnishing a role with the group for the newcomer: "Where's the doorbell? You have a visitor!" The initial guardedness of the play group disappears in light of a visitor role.

Framing Appropriate Behavior as "Play"

The value of peer play in the teacher culture of the play yard is also found in the implicit understanding of appropriate behavior. In "Two Guys," Karen speaks to Lawrence about his running. She then informs Carl and Warren of what she had just told Lawrence: "I told Lawrence that if he wanted to play with you, he should play with you and not chase you. O.K.?" Karen delivers this information with no further elaboration or explanation as to what she specifically means when she says "play with you." Carl and Warren appear to understand Karen's remarks as providing instruction and direction. Both Karen and Ken use the word *game* to refer to a notion of group activity with either explicit or implicit intention or theme. "What game are you playing?" prompts choices for appropriate behavior.

When a group of children appear intent on continued disruptive teasing of another group, Karen, having observed this activity for some time, finally addresses the teasing children: "Sarah, this is not a good game. Find some other game to play." The group moves to a different area and begins a different activity without concern, accepting the teacher's assessment of inappropriateness while supporting their play together in a new ecology.

CONCLUSION

This study illustrates how the teachers and children continually negotiate meaning within the context of peer play. The peer play episode in the play yard is a continually negotiated process between the children's play intentions and culture and the teachers' intentions and culture. As a socially and culturally organized structure in the classroom, the peer play episode involves particular and definable configurations of actions. There are stereotyped ways in which children initiate, negotiate, and enact their needs within the play episode. There are equally defined ways in which the teacher supports interactive cooperation based on the children's progression in the episode.

When and where the episode breaks down is an indication of disruption in the peer or teacher culture. In documenting the teaching of Karen and Ken, I found that a breakdown is usually a result of a disruption of the norms of peer culture. Such a breakdown may occur because of the undeveloped social skills of the children: for example, a child who is trying to be included in a play episode but doesn't understand the norms that have been developed between the children already participating in the episode. Or, in the case of Raymond and Matthew, norms that are so private and idiosyncratic between regular playmates that further shared experience is needed for others to understand them, including the teacher researcher. A breakdown in the play episode itself signals a shift or clash in cultural perspectives and accompanying values. When a disruption in the play episode occurs, teachers have a distinct opportunity to confer acknowledgment.

The degree of acknowledgment conferred by the teachers will greatly facilitate negotiation. The strategy of acknowledgment is indirect, however, and is successful to the extent that the teacher does not overtly express the teacher culture. Acknowledgment is intended to be nonintrusive, the goal being the continuation of the play episode. When an episode requires teacher support, children have the opportunity to understand the culture of the teachers and the ecological expectations. While Raymond is tentative in his alliance with Matthew, it is not appropriate for him to launch a psychological assault on Lawrence to reassure himself of his bond with

Matthew. When Marta "tells" on Warren's spoiled brat retort, Karen refocuses attention to Warren's intention and needs.

Psychological safety in the teacher culture is as much about reflecting on why a disruption has occurred as in noticing the impulsiveness. Karen explains to Lawrence, "If you want to play with Warren and Carl, you have to 'play with' them." Teachers expect physical and psychological safety and autonomous focus during pretend play with peers. Casey would like to draw Ken back into the dam-digging game, inviting him to be the architect. But Ken prefers the separation of communicating from a distant city office. Danny, Seth, Casey, and Lawrence embrace the expectation that play is focused when it is located, and it makes sense to them. They even adopt the expectation themselves. In all these circumstances the children have the opportunity to make sense of this classroom's teaching culture with the suggestions, comments, and directives delivered by teachers. A breakdown in a play episode is an opportunity for negotiation between the two cultures. The success of such negotiation is immediately assessed by whether or not the episode progresses.

Learning in the play yard occurs in the context of play with peers, in the invention and reformulation of new meanings. The teacher creates and maintains play space with respect to the shared history of peer play in each ecology, and the children transform the ecological context to their unique frame of reference. The play yard revolves around the meaning systems of the children and the teacher within the peer play episode. For the children, such meaning systems include shared and sometimes stereotypical themes and gestures, utterances, and songs; the impact of idiosyncratic personal experience with family, community, storybook, television, and movie themes; and the typical childhood themes of friendship and control. For the teacher, meaning systems involve an appreciation of one's style and the specific strategies adopted to complement and refine that style. Karen and Ken are two experienced teachers who derived meaning from my research by more clearly articulating their own particular style and the strategies reflected by that style. Teachers develop a conceptualization of their role in the peer play episode and a willingness to remain receptive to the intentions of the children through thoughtful negotiation of special rights and privileges intended to promote continued social learning.

Promoting independent outdoor play is especially important when children's lives are increasingly regulated by the company of adults as children move from the family environment into the formal structure of the education system. Outdoor play settings may be the one place where children can independently orchestrate their own negotiations with the physical and social environment and gain the clarity of selfhood necessary to navigate later in life.

References

Anderson, E. (1977). *Learning how to speak with style*. Unpublished doctoral dissertation, Stanford University, Palo Alto, California.

Aureli, T., & Coecchia, N. (1996). Day care experience and free play behavior in preschool children. *Journal of Applied Developmental Psychology, 17*, 1–17.

Bae, B. (1987, August). *Aspects of participant observation in the day care context*. Paper presented at the Symposium for Qualitative Research in Psychology, Perugia, Italy.

Bateson, G. (1976). A theory of play and fantasy. In J. S. Bruner, A. Jolly, & K. Sylva (Eds.), *Play: Its role in development and evolution* (pp. 119–129). New York: Basic Books.

Berk, L. E., & Winsler, A. (1995). *Scaffolding children's learning: Vygotsky on early childhood education*. Washington, DC: National Association for the Education of Young Children.

Blurton-Jones, N. (1976). Rough-and-tumble play among nursery school children. In J. S. Bruner, A. Jolly, & K. Sylva (Eds.), *Play: Its role in development and evolution* (pp. 352–363). New York: Basic Books.

Bodrova, E., & Leong, D. J. (1998). Adult infuences on play: The Vygotskian approach. In D. P. Fromberg & D. Bergen (Eds.), *Play from birth to twelve and beyond: Contexts, perspectives, and meanings* (pp. 277–282). New York: Garland Publishing.

Bredekamp, S., & Copple, C. (Eds.). (1997). *Developmentally appropriate practice in early childhood programs* (Rev. ed.). Washington, DC: National Association for the Education of Young Children.

Bronson, W. (1995). *The right stuff for children from birth to 8: Selecting play materials to support development*. Washington, DC: National Association for the Education of Young Children.

Carson, J., Burks, V., & Parke, R. (1993). Parent-child physical play: Determinants and consequences. In K. MacDonald (Ed.), *Parent-child play* (pp. 197–220). Albany: State University of New York Press.

Cazden, C. B. (1983). Adult assistance to language development: Scaffolds, models and direct instruction. In R. P. Parker & F. A. Davis (Eds.), *Developing literacy: Young children's use of language* (pp. 3–18). Newark, DE: International Reading Association.

Cook-Gumperz, J. (1978). *Tea partying: Recognition of naturally ordered activities*. Unpublished manuscript, University of California at Berkeley.

Cook-Gumperz, J. (1981). Persuasive talk in the social organization of children's speech. In J. Green & C. Wallat (Eds.), *Ethnography in educational settings* (pp. 25–50). Norwood, NJ: Ablex.

Cook-Gumperz, J., & Corsaro, W. (1977). Social-ecological constraints on children's communication strategies. *Sociology, 11*, 412–434.

Corsaro, W. (1979). "We're friends, right?" Children's use of access rituals in a nursery school. *Language in Society, 8*, 315–336.

Corsaro, W. (1985). *Friendship and peer culture in the early years.* Norwood, NJ: Ablex.

Corsaro, W. (1986). Routines in peer culture. In J. Cook-Gumperz, W. Corsaro, & J. Streeck (Eds.), *Children's worlds and children's language* (pp. 231–245). Berlin: Walter deGruyter & Co.

Corsaro, W. (1997). *The sociology of childhood.* Thousand Oaks, CA: Pine Forge Press.

DeVries, R., Haney, J. P., & Zan, B. (1991). Sociomoral atmosphere in direct-instruction, eclectic, and constructivist kindergartens: A study of teachers' enacted interpersonal understanding. *Early Childhood Research Quarterly, 6*, 449–471.

Dodge, D. T., & Colker, L. J. (1992). *The creative curriculum for early education* (3rd ed.). Washington DC: Teaching Strategies.

Eisert, D., & Lamprey, S. (1996). Play as a window on child development: The relationship between play and other developmental domains. *Early Education and Development, 7*(3), 221–235.

Erickson, F. (1986). Qualitative methods in research on teaching. In M. C. Wittrock (Ed.), *Handbook of research on teaching* (3rd ed.; pp. 119–161). New York: American Educational Research Association.

Erickson, E., & Mohatt, G. (1982). The cultural organization of participant structures in two classrooms of Indian students. In G. Spindler (Ed.), *Doing the ethnography of schooling* (pp. 132–174). New York: Holt, Rinehart & Winston.

Ervin-Tripp, S. (1983). *Activity structure as scaffolding for children's second language learning.* Unpublished manuscript, University of California at Berkeley.

Fein, G. G. (1985). The affective psychology of play. In C. C. Brown & A. W. Gottfried (Eds.), *Play interactions* (pp. 19–28). Skillman, NJ: Johnson & Johnson.

Fein, G. G., & Wiltz, N. W. (1998). Play as children see it. In D. P. Fromberg & D. Bergen (Eds.), *Play from birth to twelve and beyond: Contexts, perspectives, and meanings* (pp. 37–49). New York: Garland Publishing.

Florio, S., & Walsh, M. (1980). The teacher as colleague in classroom research. In H. Trueba, G. Gutherie, & K. Au (Eds.), *Culture in the bilingual classroom: Studies in classroom ethnogrphy* (pp. 87–101). Rowley, MA: Newbery House.

Fromberg, D. P. (1999). A review of research on play. In C. Seefeldt (Ed.), *The early childhood curriculum: Current findings in theory and practice* (3rd ed.; pp. 27–53). New York: Teachers College Press.

Gallas, K. (1998). *Sometimes I can be anything: Power, gender, and identity in a primary classroom.* New York: Teachers College Press.

Goffman, E. (1963). *Behavior in public places.* New York: Free Press.

Hartup, W. W., French, D. C., Laursen, B., Johnston, M. K., & Ogawa, J. R. (1993). Conflict and friendship relations in middle childhood: Behavior in a closed-field setting. *Child Development, 64*, 445–454.

Heath, S. B. (1983). *Ways with words: Language, life and work in communities and class-rooms.* New York: Cambridge University Press.

Johannessen, E. (1987). *The researcher as instrument.* Paper presented at the Symposium for Qualitative Research in Psychology, Perugia, Italy.

Jones, E., & Reynolds, G. (1992). *The play's the thing: Teacher's roles in children's play.* New York: Teachers College Press.

King, N. (1992). The impact of context on the play of young children. In S. Kessler & B. Swadener (Eds.), *Reconceptualizing the early childhood curriculum* (pp. 43–61). New York: Teachers College Press.

Levin, D. (1998). Play with violence: Understanding and responding effectively. In D. P. Fromberg & D. Bergen (Eds.), *Play from birth to twelve and beyond: Contexts, perspectives, and meanings* (pp. 348–356). New York: Garland Publishing.

Mead, G. H. (1934). *Mind, self and society.* Chicago: University of Chicago Press.

Opie, I. A., & Opie, P. (1959). *The lore and language of school children.* Oxford, England: Oxford University Press.

Paley, V. G. (1992). *You can't say you can't play.* Chicago: University of Chicago Press.

Parke, R. D., Cassidy, J., Burks, V., Carson, J., & Boyum, L. (1992). Familial contributions to peer competence among young children: The role of interactive and affective processes. In R. D. Parke & G. Ladd (Eds.), *Family-peer relationships* (pp. 107–134). Hillsdale, NJ: Erlbaum.

Pelligrini, A. D. (1982). Preschoolers' generation of cohesive text in two play contexts. *Discourse Processes, 5,* 101–107.

Pelligrini, A. D. (1993). Boys' rough-and-tumble play, social competence, and group composition. *British Journal of Developmental Psychology, 11,* 237–248.

Pelligrini, A. D. (1995). *School recess and playground behavior: Educational and developmental roles.* Albany: State University of New York Press.

Pelligrini, A. D., Huberty, P. D., & Jones, I. (1995). The effects of recess timing on children's playground and classroom behavior. *American Educational Research Journal, 32*(4), 845–864.

Pelligrini, A. D., & Smith, P. K. (1998). Physical activity play: The nature and function of a neglected aspect of play. *Child Development, 69,* 577–598.

Perry, J. P. (1989). *Teacher strategies in an early childhood play setting.* Unpublished doctoral dissertation, University of California, Berkeley.

Philips, S. U. (1982). *The invisible culture: Communication in classroom and community on the Warm Springs Reservation.* New York: Longman.

Piaget, J. (1962). *Play, dreams and imitation in childhood.* New York: Norton.

Piaget, J. (1969). *The language and thought of the child.* New York: World Publishing.

Ramsey, P. G., & Lasquade, C. (1996). Preschool children's entry attempts. *Journal of Applied Developmental Psychology, 17,* 135–150.

Reynolds, G., & Jones, E. (1997). *Master players: Learning from children at play.* New York: Teachers College Press.

Rubin, K. H., Fein, G., & Vandenberg, B. (1983). Play. In E. M. Hetherington (Ed.), *Handbook of child psychology: Vol. 4. Socialization, personality and social development.* New York: John Wiley & Sons, Inc.

Scales, B. (1984). *Strategies for the assessment of the social ecology of a preschool play environment.* Unpublished doctoral dissertation, University of California, Berkeley.

Scales, B. (1987). Play: The child's unseen curriculum. In P. Monighan-Nourot, B. Scales, J. Van Hoorn, with M. Almy. *Looking at children's play: A bridge between theory and practice* (pp. 89–115). New York: Teachers College Press.

Schultz, J. J., Florio, S., & Erickson, E. (1982). Where's the floor? Aspects of the cultural organization of social relationships in communication at home and school. In P. Gilmore & A. A. Glatthorn (Eds.), *Children in and out of school: Ethnography and education* (pp. 88–123). Washington, DC: Center for Applied Linguistics.

Smilansky, S. (1968). *The effects of sociodramatic play on disadvantaged preschool children.* New York: John Wiley & Sons, Inc.

Smilansky, S. (1990). Sociodramatic play: Its relevance to behavior and achievement in school. In E. Klugman & S. Smilansky (Eds.), *Children's play and learning: Perspectives and policy implications* (pp. 18–42). New York: Teachers College Press.

Smilansky, S., & Shefataya, L. (1990). *Facilitating play: A medium for promoting cognitive, socio-emotional and academic development in young children.* Gaithersburg, MD: Psychosocial and Educational Publications.

Sutton-Smith, B. (1985). Play research: State of the art. In J. L. Frost & S. Sunderlin (Eds.), *When children play: Proceedings of the international conference on play and play environments.* Wheaton, MD: Association for Childhood Education International.

Sutton-Smith, B., & Byrne, D. (1984). The phenomenon of bipolarity in play theories. In T. D. Yawkey & A. D. Pelligrini (Eds.), *Child's play: Developmental and applied.* Hillsdale, NJ: Erlbaum.

Trawick-Smith, J. (1988). "Let's say you're the baby, OK?" Play, leadership and following behavior of young children. *Young Children, 43*(5), 51–59.

Trawick-Smith, J. (1992). A descriptive study of persuasive preschool children: How they get others to do what they want. *Early Childhood Research Quarterly, 7*(1), 95–114.

Trawick-Smith, J. (1994). *Interactions in the classroom: Facilitating play in the early years.* Upper Saddle River, NJ: Merrill/Prentice Hall.

Trawick-Smith, J. (1998). School-based play and social interactions: Opportunities and limitations. In D. P. Fromberg & D. Bergen (Eds.), *Play from birth to twelve and beyond: Contexts, perspectives, and meanings* (pp. 241–247). New York: Garland Publishing.

Van Hoorn, J., Nourot, P., Scales, B., & Alward, K. (1999). *Play at the center of the curriculum* (2nd Ed.). Upper Saddle River, NJ: Merrill/Prentice Hall.

Vygotsky, L. S. (1967). Play and its role in the mental development of the child. *Soviet Psychology, 12,* 62–76.

Vygotsky, L. S. (1978). *Mind in society: Development of higher psychological processes.* Cambridge, MA: Harvard University Press.

Index

Accreditation, 2
Adaptability, of peer play routines, 107
Affiliation, in peer culture, 12–13
Aggression, rough-and-tumble play
    versus, 6, 73
Alward, K., 13, 16, 29, 40, 53, 57, 81
Anderson, E., 13
Animal play themes, 7
Animals, play of, 13
Approach-and-flee routine, 109–113
    function of, 111, 112–113
    in Making a New Road episode, 45–46,
        47, 52, 111–113
    in Needles episode, 27, 31–33, 39, 90,
        109–111, 113
    observable features of, 110, 112
    in Two Guys episode, 72–73, 74
Artist apprentice strategy of teacher, 82
Aureli, T., 5
Autonomous pretend play, 83
    duration of, 84
    teacher decision-making process in, 86
    teacher strategies to support, 85

Bae, Berit, 98
Bateson, Gregory, 13
"Being naughty" theme, 26
    in Needles episode, 33, 36, 38, 39–40
Berk, L. E., 57
Blurton-Jones, N., 79
Bodrova, E., 57
Boyum, L., 114
Bredekamp, S., 2
Bronson, W., 2
Burks, V., 114
Byrne, D., 30

Call of alarm, in Dam is Breaking episode,
    59–60

Carl (student)
    described, x, 69
    in Two Guys episode, 68–82
Carson, J., 114
Casey (student)
    in Dam is Breaking episode, 55–67
    described, 55
Cassidy, J., 114
Cazden, C. B., 4
Challenging authority, 26–27
    in Needles episode, 29–30
Chris (student)
    described, x, 43
    in Making a New Road episode, 43–53
Classroom
    ecology of play yard versus, 7–8
    functions of, ix–x
    teaching culture of, xii, 24–25
Climbing structure
    described, 27
    ecology of, 6–7
    in Needles episode, 27–41
    in Two Guys episode, 68–82
Coecchia, N., 5
Colker, L. J., 2
Communal sharing, in peer culture, 11
Control
    evasion of adult rules and, 30
    in peer culture, 11, 14
Cook-Gumperz, Jenny, 4, 13
Copple, C., 2
Corsaro, William, xii, 4, 11–12, 28–31, 32,
    50, 56, 69, 76, 79, 106, 110, 111
Cross-gender approach-avoidance play
    importance of, 79
    in Two Guys episode, 68–82
Cues
    interpreting environmental, 10
    open-ended, 5

Dam is Breaking episode, 54–67
    enactment stage of, 56–65
    initiation stage of, 55–56
    negotiation stage of, 56, 60
    review of, 65–67
Danger routine, 107–109
    function of, 109
    observable features of, 108–109
    in Two Guys episode, 68–82, 107–109,
        113
Danny (student)
    described, x, 43
    in Making a New Road episode, 43–53
Developmentally appropriate practice,
        play in, 2
DeVries, R., 4
Direct intervention, 84, 85, 92–103
    criteria for, 92–98
    to interrupt episode, 102–103
    to reinforce and elaborate on
        information, 101–102
    to solicit or verify information, 99–101
    types of, 98–103
Dodge, D. T., 2
Dora (student)
    in Dam is Breaking episode, 55–67
    described, x, 55, 69
    in Two Guys episode, 68–82
Duration of autonomous play, 84

Ecology
    defined, 3, 84–87
    indirect coordination of, 84–92
    of inside classroom versus play yard, 7–8
    play area as, 3–8
    preparation of, 84–88
    refinement of, 88–91
    teacher expectations in, 4–5
Enactment of themes, xii, 15
    in Dam is Breaking episode, 56–65
    loss of focus in, 94–95
    in Making a New Road episode, 45–51
    in Needles episode, 31–37
    in Two Guys episode, 72–79
Entry requests
    in Dam is Breaking episode, 56
    in Making a New Road episode, 45, 49,
        52
    in Needles episode, 29, 31–37

Erickson, E., 24
Erickson, F., xi, 24
Ervin-Tripp, Susan, 9, 57
Expectations for learning
    cues for, 4–5
    teacher, 4–5
    teacher culture and, 4–5, 114–117
Explosive theme, in Making a New Road
        episode, 50–51, 52

Familial/house themes, 7
Feigned fear
    in Needles episode, 39
    in Two Guys episode, 76
Fein, G. G., 5, 8, 114
Field note information, xii
Florio, S., 24
Focused pretend play
    as goal for teacher, 83–84
    loss of focus in, 92–95
French, D. C., 6
Friendship, in peer culture, 12–13
Fromberg, Doris P., 3, 6, 21, 83–84, 109,
        114

Gallas, Karen, 13, 24–25, 39, 56, 59, 96
Group fantasy play, 8–15
    features of, 8–9, 80–81
    language skills in, 9, 10, 13
    in Making a New Road episode, 42–53
    in Needles episode, 26–41
    peer culture in, 10–11, 105–114
    shift between reality and fantasy in, 9
    social development in, 6, 10–11, 14–15,
        16
    structure of, 9
Guardian of the gate role of teacher, in
        Needles episode, 40–41

Haney, J. P., 4
Harold E. Jones Child Study Center
    (University of California, Berkeley)
    classroom use in, ix–x
    pretend play and, x–xii
    student subjects in, x
    teacher subjects in, x
Hartup, W. W., 6
Heath, S. B., 24
Huberty, P. D., 4

Imaginary place, creation of, 21–22, 87–88
Indirect coordination of ecology, 84–92
  indirect support of ongoing play, 91–92
  preparation of ecology, 84–88
  refinement of ecology, 88–91
Initiation of play, xii, 14–15
  in Dam is Breaking episode, 55–56
  loss of focus in, 92–93
  in Making a New Road episode, 43–44
  in Needles episode, 27–31
  in Two Guys episode, 69–72

Johannessen, E., xi
Johnston, M. K., 6
Jones, E., 16, 40, 53, 114
Jones, I., 4

Karen (teacher)
  described, x
  in Making a New Road episode, 42–53
  observer role and, 19–21, 23–24, 42–53, 69–82
  organizer role of, 42–53
  profile of, 19–21
  in Two Guys episode, 68–82
Ken (teacher)
  described, x
  in Needles episode, 31–40
  in negotiation of play, 29, 31–37
  observer role and, 63–67
  organizer role and, 21–24, 54–67
  profile of, 21–24
King, N., 4

Language skills, in group fantasy play, 9, 10, 13
Lasquade, C., 5
Laursen, B., 6
Lawrence (student)
  in Dam is Breaking episode, 55–67
  described, x, 27, 43, 55, 69
  in Making a New Road episode, 43–53
  in Needles episode, 26–41
  in Two Guys episode, 68–82
Leong, D. J., 57
"Let's hide" theme, in Needles episode, 28–29
Levin, Diane, 2

Localization of play groups, 88
"Look at me" theme, in Needles episode, 27–28

Making a New Road episode, 42–53
  approach-and-flee routine in, 45–46, 47, 52, 111–113
  enactment stage of, 45–51
  initiation stage of, 43–44
  negotiation stage of, 43–44, 51
  review of, 52–53
Marta (student)
  described, x, 69
  in Two Guys episode, 68–82
Matthew (student)
  described, x, 27
  in Needles episode, 26–41
Mead, George Herbert, 28, 38
Mediation role, in Making a New Road episode, 53
Mentor theme, in Making a New Road episode, 48
Methodological notes, xii
Mohatt, G., 24
Mutuality, in peer play routines, 106

Needles episode, 26–41
  approach-and-flee routine in, 27, 31–33, 39, 90, 109–111, 113
  enactment stage of, 31–37
  initiation stage of, 27–31
  negotiation stage of, 27–31
  review of, 38–41
Negotiation of play, xii, 15
  in Dam is Breaking episode, 56, 60
  dyads versus triads and, 28–40
  loss of focus in, 93–94
  in Making a New Road episode, 43–44, 51
  in Needles episode, 27–31
  teacher and, 29, 31–37
  in Two Guys episode, 69–72
Nourot, P., 13, 16, 29, 40, 53, 57, 81

Observer role of teacher
  described, 17–19
  Karen (teacher) and, 19–21, 23–24, 42–53, 69–82
  Ken (teacher) and, 63–67

Observer role of teacher (*continued*)
 in Needles episode, 40
 rich information and, 20–21
 in Two Guys episode, 68–82
Ogawa, J. R., 6
Onlooker role
 in Dam is Breaking episode, 63–67
 in Making a New Road episode, 50,
  52
Opie, I. A., 56
Opie, P., 56
Organizer role of teacher
 described, 17
 Karen (teacher) and, 42–53
 Ken (teacher) and, 21–24, 54–67
Outer space play, 22

Paley, V. G., 4, 13
Parke, R. D., 114
Peacemaker role of teacher
 in Needles episode, 40
 in Two Guys episode, 81–82
Peer culture. *See also* Group fantasy play
 children's play as, 10–11
 communal sharing in, 11
 control in, 11, 14
 development of social competence in,
  13–14
 power in, 14
 rituals and routines in, 11–14, 38, 105,
  106
Peer play routines, xii, 105–114
 approach-and-flee routine, 109–113
 characteristics of, 106–107
 cultural manifestations of, 2–3
 danger routine, 68–82, 107–109, 113
 function of, 107, 109, 111, 112–113
 supervising, 113–114
Pelligrini, A. D., 4, 6, 57, 73, 114
Perry, J. P., xi
Perspective taking, 10
Philips, Susan U., 24
Physical safety, 95–96
Piaget, Jean, 46
Play episodes
 Dam is Breaking episode, 54–67
 Making a New Road episode, 42–53
 Needles episode, 26–41
 primacy of, 82
 Two Guys episode, 68–82

Playmate choice
 entry requests and, 29, 31–37, 45, 49, 52,
  56
 importance of, 116
Play tutor, teacher as, 40, 66–67
Play yard
 climbing structure in, 6–7, 27–41, 68–
  82
 as complex learning environment, 5–8
 distinctions between pretend and real
  in, 6
 as ecology, 3–8
 ecology of classroom versus, 7–8
 in Needles episode, 26–41
 open-field ecologies, 6
 props in, 5, 6
 sand pit in, 6, 42–43, 54–67, 87
Power, in peer culture, 14
Pretend play
 in developmentally appropriate
  practice, 2
 with peers. *See* Group fantasy play
 shift between reality and, 9, 37, 66
 teacher support of, x–xii, 1–3
Problem solving, in group fantasy play,
 10
Promoter role of teacher
 described, 19
 Ken (teacher) and, 21–24
Props, 5, 6
 in Dam is Breaking episode, 57–65
 in Making a New Road episode, 44–53
Protector role, in Making a New Road
 episode, 53
Psychological safety, 96–98

Ramsey, P. G., 5
Raymond (student)
 in Dam is Breaking episode, 55–67
 described, x, 27, 55
 in Needles episode, 26–41
Reality, shift between fantasy and, 9, 37,
 66
Repetition, in peer routines, 105, 106
Representational thinking, in group
 fantasy play, 10
Restoration role, in Making a New Road
 episode, 53
Retaliatory theme, in Needles episode, 34–
 35

Review of episode
Dam is Breaking episode, 65–67
Making a New Road, 52–53
Needles episode, 38–41
Two Guys episode, 79–82
Reynolds, G., 16, 40, 53, 114
Rituals, in peer play routines, 11–14, 38,
105, 106
Robert (student)
in Dam is Breaking episode, 55–67
described, 55
Role assignments, in Dam is Breaking
episode, 63–64, 66
Rough-and-tumble play
aggression versus, 6, 73
in Two Guys episode, 68–82
Routines, in peer culture, 11–14, 38, 105, 106
Rubin, K. H., 8
Running routine
in Needles episode, 30–31
in Two Guys episode, 75

Safety, 95–98
physical, 95–96
psychological, 96–98
Sand kitchen routines, in Needles episode,
37, 38, 40
Sand pit
in Dam is Breaking episode, 54–67
ecology of, 6, 87
in Making a New Road episode, 42–53
Scaffolding, in Dam is Breaking episode, 57
Scales, Barbara, ix, 3–6, 13–16, 29, 40, 53,
57, 81, 82
Schultz, J. J., 24
Scripts, 5
Separation of play groups, 88–90
Seth (student)
described, x, 43
in Making a New Road episode, 43–53
Smilansky, Sara, 8–9, 16–17, 20, 40, 66, 80–
81
Smith, P. K., 6, 73, 114
Social and cultural organization of
classroom
components of, 105
peer play routines in, 105–114
Social development
interactions with peers and, 28
play in support of, 6, 10–11, 14–15, 16

Space
possession of, in play yard, 114–116
preparation of, 87
reference to, 90
Staff conversations, xii
Suggestive features, 4–5
Superhero themes, 7
Sutton-Smith, B., 30

Tangletalk, in Dam is Breaking episode,
55–56, 65
Teacher(s)
alternating teaching days of, xi
challenging authority of, 26–27, 29–30
concept of teacher, 3
facilitation techniques of, 16–17
guardian of the gate role of, 40–41
in negotiation of play, 29, 31–37
observer role of. *See* Observer role of
teacher
organizer role of, 17, 21–24, 42–67
peacemaker role of, 40, 81–82
as play tutors, 40, 66–67
profiles of, 19–24
promoter role of, 19, 21–24
roles of, 16–19, 113–114
supervision of peer play routines, 113–
114
support of pretend play, x–xii, 1–3
understanding of sequence of games,
15
Teacher culture
and expectations for valued behavior, 4–
5, 114–117
inside classroom, xii, 24–25
Teacher strategies, xii, 16–17, 83–103
artist apprentice, 82
continuum of, 81
direct intervention in play episode, 84,
85, 92–103
goals and, 83–84
indirect coordination of ecology, 84–92
Themes of play
elaboration of, 91
enactment of, xii
organizer role of teacher and, 21–24
types of, 7
Theoretical notes, xii
Threat theme, in Needles episode, 32–33,
34–35, 39, 40

Trawick-Smith, J., 4–6, 13, 16–17, 40, 53
Turn taking, in group fantasy play, 10
Two Guys episode, 68–82
    approach-and-flee routine in, 72–73, 74
    danger routine in, 68–82, 107–109, 113
    enactment stage of, 72–79
    framing behavior as "play," 116–117
    initiation stage of, 69–72
    negotiation stage of, 69–72
    primacy of play episode, 82
    review of, 79–82
    rough-and-tumble play in, 68–82

Unusual events, xii

Vandenberg, B., 8
Van Hoorn, J., 13, 16, 29, 40, 53, 57, 81

Verbal markers, in Making a New Road
    episode, 44
Videotape coding, xi
Vocal quality, in peer culture, 13
Voice tone, 105
Vygotsky, Lev, 10, 48

Walsh, M., 24
Warren (student)
    described, x, 69
    in Two Guys episode, 68–82
Water theme, in Dam is Breaking episode,
    54–67
Wiltz, N. W., 5
Winsler, A., 57

Zan, B., 4

ABOUT THE AUTHOR

Jane P. Perry is the research coordinator and a teacher at the Harold E. Jones Child Study Center at the Institute of Human Development, University of California, Berkeley. She has a Ph.D. from the University of California, Berkeley, an M.A. from the University of Minnesota, and a B.A. from McGill University. She is also a technical writer for the California Early Childhood Mentor Program, which improves child care through mentorship, salary enhancement, career development, and leadership. She has been an adjunct instructor in early childhood care and education, and currently sits on the Committee to Get the Word Out at the Institute of Human Development, with the aim of bringing results of studies in human development to professional and lay communities.

She also writes short fiction on the topic of motherhood. Her story "Lacto-Babe" appeared in *The Mother Is Me* (1998).